GARDINER C. MEANS

Institutionalist and Post Keynesian

GARDINER C. MEANS Institutionalist and Post Keynesian

Warren J. Samuels
Michigan State University

and

Steven G. Medema
University of Colorado at Denver

M. E. Sharpe, Inc.
Armonk, New York ▪ London, England

Available in the United Kingdom and Europe from M. E. Sharpe, Publishers, 3 Henrietta Street, London WC2E 8LU.

Library of Congress Cataloging-in-Publication Data

Samuels, Warren J., 1933–
Gardiner C. Means: institutionalist and post Keynesian / by Warren J. Samuels and Steven G. Medema.
p. cm.
ISBN 0-87332-615-6 : ISBN 0-87332-616-4 (pbk.)
1. Means, Gardiner Coit, 1896– . 2. Institutional economics. 3. Keynesian economics. I. Medema, Steven G. II. Title.
HB119.M43S36 1990
330.1—dc20 90-30976
CIP

Printed in the United States of America

∞

ED 10 9 8 7 6 5 4 3 2 1

To Sylvia and Debra

Contents

Preface

The authors are profoundly indebted to Caroline F. Ware, Frederic S. Lee, and John Munkirs for materials and insights not otherwise obtainable. Professor Lee has been especially generous in sharing materials which he has collected from various archival and other sources as well as his own manuscripts. He also was both very helpful in offering suggestions for revision of an early draft of this book and very sympathetic in regard to differences in interpretive nuance (indeed, the reader may find the several points of interpretive difference of some interest). Caroline Ware has been most helpful in providing various materials and in responding to questions about her late husband. She has also been most gracious in differing with us in the interpretation of Means as Post Keynesian and Institutionalist, noted in chapter 5. We are indebted to John Wisman of American University, and to Vivian Wiser and Thomas S. Shorebird of the Economic Research Service and the Graduate School, respectively, of the United States Department of Agriculture, for information concerning Gardiner Means's teaching activities at American University and the Graduate School. We are also indebted to colleagues in the Department of Economics, Michigan State University, for instructive discussions pertaining to Gardiner Means and his work. Not least we are indebted to John Pheby for the initial stimulation which led to this work.

Some indication of the scope and direction of this study can be achieved by examining the table of contents. We treat Gardiner C. Means as economic theorist, empiricist, paradigm creator, and policy theorist, with principal attention to what we consider his thinking of deepest and permanent consequence. We do *not* attempt to accomplish several things also of importance, including (1) an intellectual biography of Means; (2) the evolution of Means's policy analysis, particularly with regard to industrial structure, recession, inflation, and stagflation; and (3) the econometric and rhetorical evaluation of the enormous literature defending, using, and criticizing Means's empirical work on concentration, administered pricing, inflation, and so on.

GARDINER C. MEANS
Institutionalist and Post Keynesian

1

Introduction

1. Introduction and Objectives

Gardiner Coit Means died 15 February 1988 at the age of ninety-one. A man of continuous activity in the public arena and not a professional academic, Means was one of the leading and most conspicuous economists of Franklin Roosevelt's New Deal. Scholars will long remember him as the co-author, with Adolf A. Berle, Jr., of one of the truly epochal books of the twentieth century, *The Modern Corporation and Private Property* (1932). In terms of the impact which this volume has had on people's understanding of the modern economy, it is in the same class with John Maynard Keynes's *General Theory of Employment, Interest and Money* (1936)—and indeed the relationship of Means's theories to those of Keynes is one facet in the historic interest of Means.

The purpose of this book is to interpret and assess the contributions of Gardiner Means to the development of economic thought. It is intended to be neither a comprehensive intellectual biography nor a mere summary of his ideas. Means's significance rests on his fundamental conceptions of the organization and control of the economic system *qua* system, especially as a system of power; and of the operation of the economy at the micro- and macroeconomic levels within that system. Means's holism, his focus on the problem of organization and control, and his deep analysis of the corporation as the distinctive major institution of the modern economy, identify his work as institutionalist. His analyses of the structural microeconomic foundations of macroeconomic performance, including the dual economy of market and administered sectors, and of the nature and limits of the microeconomic and macroeconomic adjustment (or coordination) processes, mark his work as a Post Keynesian economist, indeed, as perhaps the *first* Post Keynesian economist. Accordingly, an interpretation and assessment of Means must relate his work to that of such distinguished economists as Keynes, Schumpeter, John Kenneth Galbraith, Alfred Eichner, and, perhaps most surprisingly, Ronald A. Coase.[1] Also, Means's ideas concerning price flexibility are of considerable importance for the interpretation of Keynes (though we shall not enter into the discussion of "what Keynes really meant" except tangentially).

Means's career also yields insight, as we shall see, into a number of areas. First, there is the enormous importance of the interpretive paradigm and other sociological factors for the status and significance of a body of ideas. In part this involves the differential and broad versus a narrow paradigmatic formulation of questions. Second, selective normative premises affect the precise form in which ideas are held (especially, in Means's case in regard to the theory of the firm). Third, we shall see alternative subtle nuances of what being a conservative in economics can involve. Fourth, there is the role played by filtration mechanisms in economics in formulating, removing, marginalizing, or sanitizing radical ideas (most notably Means's doctrine of administered prices). Fifth, we shall see how several factors influenced the reception and evaluation of Means's work: economic and political ideology; methodological disciplinary emphasis on a priori theory rather than messy empiricism; substantive disciplinary emphasis on the Walrasian competitive model; the Keynesian revolution; the sociological (in-group, out-group) structure of the discipline; the privileged position given to the received paradigm; and the diversity of reception and evaluation resulting from diversity within economics, an economics whose basis for interpretation cannot properly be reduced solely to one school, whether that be Chicago or Post

Keynesian economics. (It will surprise no one that conservative economists fought what they perceived to be Means's attack on the capitalist market economy and that liberal economists found reinforcement for various reformist schemes.) Finally, we shall see that the core of Means's ideas—the corporate system and administered pricing—have ramifications which reverberate throughout all the important dimensions of economics and which fundamentally conflict with more orthodox ideas in every respect.

In the process we shall interpretively comment on the status of various controversies involving his work. One of the interpretive complications arises from the fact that Means's central ideas, which remained fundamentally intact throughout his adult life, were frequently more or less slightly reformulated in response to both criticism and changing circumstances and also his selective absorption of others' ideas—for example, those of Keynes and Edward H. Chamberlin, with which he understood his own to compete. Not unlike many other writers, Means focused on and gave great weight to his own ideas, but, like too few others, he also declined to make them the exclusive explanation of relevant phenomena—although he was often perceived as advocating monistic ideas. We shall focus on what we consider the central operative thrust of his ideas, rather than on specific formulations—although in several cases we do pay attention to or at least acknowledge the varying formulations. The reader should be aware that the scope of the present volume prevents detailed consideration of the enormous literature that has developed on the many topics on which Means worked—even limited to those dealing with his work alone, most notably on the statistics of administered pricing and on the meaning and significance of the separation of ownership and control.

Chapter 1 examines the facets of significance attached to Means's work, the problem of interpretation, a precis of his career, and his general perspective. Chapter 2 treats Means's conception of the corporate system, including the modern corporation, private property, and the economy as a system of power. Chapter 3 examines Means's approach to microeconomics, including his theories of administered pricing, the price adjustment process, and the firm in relation to the market. Chapter 4 examines the macroeconomic consequences of administered pricing, including the relation of his ideas to Say's Law and Keynes's and Post Keynesian macroeconomics. Chapter 5 offers a necessarily cursory assessment of the reception given Means's ideas and the relation of his work to that of others. Chapter 6 further assesses the place and significance of Gardiner Means in the history of economic thought.

2. The Problem of Interpretation

It is now widely appreciated that economics is a story-telling discipline, a system of belief rather than of hard, unequivocal science. Some of these stories are orthodox, a function of the professional dominance of a certain school and/or of ideological congruity. Others are heterodox. Yet orthodoxy is itself diverse, and elements of stories which appear radical in heterodox stories are present in more orthodox stories in more or less sanitized versions. It is principally in the most ideological or extreme of the orthodox stories that these heterodox elements are either ignored or more or less ostentatiously rejected, in the latter respect honored, as it were, by the attention given them in order to present a story of conclusive rebuttal. This description fits the ideas of Gardiner Means, the reception and status of whose ideas have very much been influenced by the positions within either a diverse orthodoxy or heterodoxy of the several commentators.

But this means that interpretation and assessment is at least in part a function of perspective. Evaluation tends to give effect to and be tautological with the premises of the interpreter's standpoint. The future status of Gardiner Means within the discipline and within the written histories of economic thought, will depend on which school, and which faction of the school, has hegemonic standing in the discipline. Already, in the present, the evaluation of his work, for example, with regard to administered pricing and its implications, depends (to use Joseph Schumpeter's phrase) upon social locational factors. This volume is written within the combined institutionalist and Post Keynesian paradigms and interprets and assesses Means in such heterodox terms and does so affirmatively.

While the precise evaluation of Means's ideas is a matter of selective perception, less equivocal are the subjects with respect to which Means's significance must be understood—though the status of the subjects will vary from school to school and to some extent within schools. These facets of significance include: the fundamental conception of the organization and control of the economic system *qua* system, especially as a system of power; and the operation of the economy at the microeconomic and macroeconomic levels, including the determination of what profit maximization means in practice, the nature and limits of the price adjustment-coordination process, the operation of the firm in relation to the market, and the microeconomic foundations of the macroeconomy and their consequences for instability.

3. A Precis of Means's Career

Means's early career was highlighted by a B.A. "war" degree in chemistry from Harvard in 1918 (coming with one semester's studies remaining); service as an army pilot during World War I; work on Near East Relief in Turkey, 1919–1920; operating his own textile manufacturing firm, 1922–1929; graduate work at Harvard, leading to the M.A. in 1927 and Ph.D. in 1933, with his doctoral dissertation not surprisingly dealing with the corporate revolution; and research work at Columbia law school, 1927–1933, where he co-authored *The Holding Company: Its Public Significance and its Regulation* (1932) with James C. Bonbright, as well as *The Modern Corporation and Private Property*—both published in the same year—arguably the most eminently productive six-year research associateship in the history of the discipline.

Means was next employed in a succession of positions in the federal government, including: economic advisor for finance to the secretary of agriculture, Henry Wallace (1933–1935); member of the Consumer Advisory Board of the National Recovery Administration (1933–1935);[2] director, Industrial Section, National Resources Committee (1935–1939); economic advisor, National Resources Planning Board (1939–1940); and fiscal analyst, Bureau of the Budget (1940–1941). He subsequently was associated with the Committee for Economic Development (CED) (1943–1958) and the Fund for the Republic (1957–1959). During the period 1951–1963 he was involved in his own lawn grass (zoysia) development company. He subsequently was an independent consultant and author.

The other volumes which Means either wrote or edited dealt principally with structural aspects of the American economy and their implications: *Patterns of Resource Use* (1938), *The Structure of the American Economy* (1939), *Pricing Power and the Public Interest* (1962b), *The Corporate Revolution in America* (1962a).[3] He was a major contributor to *The Roots of Inflation*, edited by John Blair et al. (1975). He published with Caroline F. Ware *The Modern Economy in Action* (1936). Special notice must be taken of his historic pamphlet *Industrial Prices and Their Relative Inflexibility* (1935) in which the difference between agricultural and industrial prices and between groups of industrial prices with regard to relative flexibility was examined. Means also published a number of articles in professional journals and in the proceedings volumes of congressional hearings, the latter generally dealing with administered pricing and its microeconomic and macroeconomic consequences.

Means was honored with the Veblen-Commons Award by the Association for Evolutionary Economics in 1974.[4]

4. Means's General Perspective

Turning to Means's general perspective and hence to the question of theory in relation to reality, we note first that Robert Heilbroner (1988, pp. 22–23) has identified a remarkable feature of modern market economies, namely, the "decisive change . . . in the manner in which social controls over behavior are *perceived*. . . . The economy appears as an autonomous process, wholly independent of the society within which it operates.''

One example of this process of perception is the standard view that markets produce Pareto-optimal results. Actually there is no unique Pareto-optimal result, only results specific to the entitlement or power structures which give rise to them. But professional practice and cultural ideological preconceptions lead us to perceive or to stress only the market process and its optimizing result, whereas in fact the market only gives effect to the power structure which forms, operates through, and channels the market.

Another example is the pervasive constrained maximization mode of analysis in economics in which individual agents are said to make choices within their opportunity sets so as to maximize utility, profit, or other advantage. This practice obscures the processes by which both the structure of opportunity sets and the substance of individual objective functions are formed, by making maximization the *starting point* of the analysis. In all these respects economic reality may be said to be either different from or much more complex than what is recognized by economic theory and economic ideology. Trade between giants and between giants and pygmies is treated as no different from that between pygmies. Both power and other social relationships are, through reification, obscured by the imagery of pure, autonomous, and automatic market forces.

This was essentially the view held by Gardiner Means.[5] From the very beginning of his thinking about economic matters, some of it based on his experience in Turkey, Means perceived that economic theory manifested a rather myopic vision of the market economy. Details of this perception will be explored below, but the general insight was that twentieth-century economists take for granted a certain institutionalization of the capitalist market economy that is radically different from that in place in both earlier periods and different areas. In the modern economy prices are set by sellers in their formation of contracts which, typically, the buyer either accepts or rejects but to which the buyer can add nothing substantive through bargaining (called contracts of adhesion or standardized contracts). The corporate stockholder in the modern economy is the passive recipient of dividends without the legal rights and opportunities earlier accorded ownership. In one respect these features are taken to constitute the essence of capitalist markets both past and present, whereas they represent major changes in the system. In another respect we perceive these features as if they comported with images of pure market price formation and the stockholder-as-ultimate-power-holder—which means that we perceive neither the adhesion (rather than bargaining) nature of contracts nor the passive nature of stockholding.

Means repeatedly lamented over economists' lack of attention to changes in important institutional details which represented major changes in the structure of the economy. He objected to the huge gap between theory—especially its emphasis upon Smithian atomistic competition as being descriptively accurate—and reality; and to the mechanistic determinism of neoclassical theory which focused on the hypothetical, the logical, and the presumptively optimal in contrast to empirical institutional complexity.[6] He saw economics dominated by mechanistic deductive elegance and by a seeming belief in an independent metaphysical order both transcending and rendering almost completely nugatory the actual phenomena and processes through which people live as economic actors. He objected above all to the exclusion and obfuscation by economic theory of the actuality of power, of the market process structured and moved by power play among economic actors with unequal resources. He had, as Bernard Nossiter (1962, p. 27) has remarked, "a taste for examining the economy as it is rather than as it ought to behave according to orthodox precepts," and was not an economist who "wrestled to fit facts to orthodox theory." As Means expressed the matter, through his undergraduate study of chemistry he "received a heavy indoctrination in the scientific method, which makes theory grow out of the results of observation and constantly tests that theory through new observations'' (Means 1975, p. 149). Accordingly, Means believed that his conception of what constitutes ''scientific analysis'' differed from the neoclassical conception, or at least its practice.

Apropos of the question of reality versus theory, it is interesting (especially in light of what we have to say in chapter 3 about the relationships between Means's and Coase's theories of the firm) that what Coase says about pricing theory based on welfare economic reasoning also applies to Means in regard to administered or full cost or markup pricing:[7]

> Marginal cost pricing as a policy is largely without merit. How then can one explain the widespread support that it has enjoyed in the economics profession? I believe it is the result of economists using an approach which I have termed ''blackboard economics.'' The policy under consideration is one which is implemented on the blackboard. All the information needed is assumed to be available and the teacher plays all the parts. . . . But there is no counterpart to the teacher within the real economic system. There is no one who is entrusted with the task that is performed on the blackboard. (Coase 1988, p. 19)

This statement is particularly striking coming from a distinguished member of the Chicago School, a group (led in this matter, of course, by George Stigler) which has been foremost in the attempt to refute or discredit Means's ideas.

But what is ''economic reality?'' Is it the abstract mechanics of market forces, of demand and supply? Or is it corporate managerial decision making as to what ''profit maximization'' involves, coupled, for example, with selective but intensive corporate interests (in contrast with other diffuse interests) in the adoption and application of certain government policies? Is it corporate executives discussing ''business,'' or something metaphysical or more abstract with respect thereto? Did ''economic reality'' change in any truly fundamental way when the economy was transformed by the corporation? What is the essential or relevant meaning of ''competition?'' Does the dichotomy of ''private'' and ''public'' make sense? Is it exhaustive, or is it even meaningful to disaggregate "private" into personal-individual and corporate-collective? Can prices meaningfully be understood to emerge in the "market," which after all is a metaphor, or need they be understood at the level of the day-to-day decision making of corporate administrators? Ultimately it is questions like these which affect the reception and evaluation of Means's ideas. In these and perhaps other respects this volume is an exercise in both (1) the interpretation and assessment of Means's ideas and (2) the analysis of the role of such considerations as those listed in this paragraph in interpretation and assessment.

The focus of Means's attention was of course the corporation and the economic process which it dominated. In the statement of his "Principal Contributions" which Means prepared for Mark Blaug's *Who's Who in Economics* (Blaug 1986, p. 588), he contrasted his experiences in preindustrial Turkey with his small textile enterprise, indicating that he "learned how little economic theory had adjusted to the basic structural changes brought to Adam Smith's economy by the modern corporation." Means included among his principal contributions "(1) showing the dominant role of the modern corporation; (2) showing the separation of ownership and control which facilitated economic concentration; (3) showing the inflexibility of administered prices which undermined the automatic mechanism traditionally relied on to maintain full employment; (4) delineating the structure of the American economy; . . ."

As early as his Harvard doctoral dissertation, "The Corporate Revolution" (1933), in *The Modern Corporation and Private Property*, and in a succession of subsequent writings, Means insisted on the importance of (1) the growth of the corporation and the corporate system, (2) the growth of big business, (3) the concentration of economic power, (4) the increasing dispersion of stock ownership, and (5) the separation of ownership and control, including the evolution of forms of control separate from ownership. On the basis of these changes he (and Berle) perceived changes in the traditional logics of property and of profits and the inadequacy of traditional legal and economic theory. Apropos of the latter, Means criticized "four major postulates of received economic theory—the trading character of the market, the determinacy of cost, the unity of the process of real saving, and the efficacy of the profit motive." He argued that they should be replaced "insofar as corporate enterprise is concerned, with (1) the administrative character of the market, (2) the indeterminacy of costs, (3) the duality of the process of saving, and finally (4) the possible ineffectiveness of 'profits' as a motivating force" (Means 1962a, p. 16).

Means thus persistently challenged traditional beliefs about the market economy and its operation and performance. He averred that we had an administered market system, or a combination of market and administration as an economic system; that a critical feature of this system was administered pricing; that economic reality in the corporate system differed radically from the traditional theory of private property, especially in regard to passive stock ownership and the separation of ownership and control; that administered pricing profoundly affected the stability of the macroeconomy, and so on. Not surprisingly, he concluded, for example, that

> when administered prices are introduced as basic assumptions, the system of theory [the classical theory developed by Smith, Mill and Marshall] is *shattered.* It will no longer yield the classical conclusions that the free enterprise system is a cybernetic mechanism which (1) automatically tends to eliminate unemployment, (2) automatically tends to balance international payments, (3) automatically tends to minimize waste and direct resources into their most appropriate uses, and (4) automatically tends to reward workers and investors and managers in proportion to the value of their productive contributions. (Means to Jerry Cohen, 20 March 1964, p. 1)

Lest one consider these thoughts unduly radical, it should be noted that the concluding section (p. 8) of the letter just quoted contains Means's statement that how far allocative and distributional distortions "are the result of pricing power as such and to what extent they are facilitated by the use of administered prices is not clear and is probably not important, at least if one accepts the proposition that administered prices are essential to efficient modern business.'' Administered pricing and the other accompaniments of the corporate system were not, to Means, something to be castigated and fought but rather features to be reckoned with in both understanding and making policy for the economy as it is, and were certainly not to be whitewashed through the use of obfuscating tautologies.

These themes, beliefs, and challenges, which constitute Means's general perspective, reduce to his conception of the corporate system and the new microeconomics and new macroeconomics applicable to the new system.

2

The Modern Corporation: Property and Power

1. Introduction

Gardiner Means believed that the economy of the United States during the century prior to the Great Depression had undergone a fundamental transformation, and the features of that transformation were still intensifying. Although the terms, such as "private property," used to describe the economy were the same as before, the existential reality to which they referred had profoundly changed. An economy of relatively small, local private enterprises had in large part been replaced by national corporations. The result was a dual economy. Moreover, the corporations had become giants, and the industrial wealth of the country had been, and was continuing to be, increasingly concentrated in a small number of corporations—a couple of hundred. This corporatization of the economy had been helped along by the transformation of stock ownership and the rise of the organized stock market which led to the dispersion of stock ownership and the effective separation of the ownership and managerial control of the corporation. What had been property arrangements involving active, vital, and direct ownership and participation in decision making had been transformed into the passive receipt of dividends. What had been an economy dominated by individual trading-bargaining behavior and market forces had been transformed into an economy of standardized contracts of adhesion and joint but rivalrous coordination by market and by administration.

To some extent these transformations had been unintended and unforeseen, but to a significant degree they were the direct and intended result of changes in the law of corporations, especially the law governing management-stockholder relations. Capitalism had, it seemed, been socialized from within, and the socializers had been the corporate officers and their lawyers as well as compliant legislators and judges.[8]

Means accepted this transformation, in part because he believed that it was the only way in which modern production and exchange could be undertaken due to the size of population and markets and also technology. But he also believed that public policy had to deal straightforwardly with the consequences of this and not be diverted by an ideology no longer applicable to the new reality, an ideology now serving to mask or obfuscate the true nature of the economy as a system of power.

Some comments on each of the components of this set of beliefs will be made below. But it is critically important to recognize from the beginning that Means was *not* saying that the market had been replaced by a corporate administered economy. He argued, rather, that the economy was best described as sectoral dualism with one sector characterized by traditional competition between small, autonomous, and especially individually owned private enterprises disciplined in traditional ways by the market; and the other by corporate giantism and concentrated production in which market and administration coexisted. The corporate sector substantially modified and to some extent replaced the market, which was manipulated by the concentrated power of corporations and the corporate sector, though it was also true that the corporate sector was itself limited by market forces. At the very least, the market was formed and its operation channeled by the structure and operation of the corporate sector. This represents a substantial departure from the picture portrayed by much conventional economic theory in which systemic and especially structural considerations are typically ignored, or at best muted, and everything is generally subsumed by transcendental "market forces." As we shall see in chapter 3, this view is, surprisingly and ironically, except in one fundamental respect, essentially identical with what has come to be the Coasian, Chicago theory of the firm.

2. The Corporation

The conventional treatment of the corporation on an analytical par with the individual household consumer, was anathema to Means because it constituted a gross misrepresentation of the modern economy. A small but important percentage of U.S. corporations have value added, assets, sales, profits, and other measures of activity equal to the gross national products (and comparable indices) of numerous nation-states, even among the developed countries. Collectively these constitute a major percentage of domestic U.S. gross national product. The first paragraph of *The Modern Corporation and Private Property* commenced with the sentences,

> Corporations have ceased to be merely legal devices through which the private business transactions of individuals may be carried on. Though still much used for this purpose, the corporate form has acquired a larger significance. The corporation has, in fact, become both a method of property tenure and a means of organizing economic life. (Berle and Means 1932, p. 1)

Means considered this to have encompassed "a change in the fundamental character of economic organization which has been brought about through the growth of corporate activity . . ." (Means 1962a, p. 15).

Considered empirically, this judgment of Means was surely correct. John R. Commons was also surely correct when he identified "the central problem dealt with by Berle and Means" as "the emergence of corporations out of individual enterprises and their domination over American life" and the corporation as "a special case'' of ''maneuvered collective action'' in which ''the millions of stockholders and bondholders . . . are marshalled by the controlling management towards collective action in perpetuating the existence and supremacy of the entity'' (Commons 1950, p. 299). Keynes argued that people live their lives in a series of short runs rather than in the long run. Means argued that people live their lives in a world largely organized into corporations. Corporations thus become, along with the modern state, the distinctive institution of the contemporary economy, a principal form of collective action, the major structural characteristic of the private sector, a fundamental way in which economic life is organized and controlled.

Means's identification of the corporation as the major ''private'' institution in the organization and control of the economy must be taken as constituting principally a positive proposition. Although his own policy position (which requires more than an ''is'' statement—an ''ought'' one as well) did not reject the corporation, his emphasis on the corporation was unwelcome for many. These included those who saw no analytical difference between the corporation and the traditional individual enterprise and household, and those who believed that such an identification of the corporation would contribute to efforts to reform the institution. For the latter group, once the corporation came to be seen as so important, more attention would be given it, a situation anathema also to those who prefer not to have their power recognized as such. The two views coalesced in a denial of the power of the corporation as an institution. The effect, if realized, would be to have treated the corporation as if it were unimportant, thus reinforcing by obfuscation the power of the corporation and those in control thereof. In this respect, at least, positive analysis is laden with normative meaning—a variant on the more general proposition that science inevitably has a political coefficient of meaning.

If Means's identification of the corporation as the dominant institution of modern economic life was unwelcome to many, his, and Berle's, further articulation of the reality of the corporate system as a form of collective capitalism was even more alien. But before we consider the idea of the corporate system we need to examine the three aspects of the "corporate revolution" stressed by Means, and of course by Berle.

3. Concentration and Size

The rise of the corporation as the premier unit of economic organization was accompanied by the combined and interrelated phenomena of corporate giantism and industrial concentration. A relative handful of modern corporations, two hundred, held almost half the assets in the 1920s and received over 40 percent of all corporate income (Berle and Means 1932, chapter 3). Three decades later, Means saw no reason to alter his description, emphasizing instead that the "three trends of economic development envisaged in the original edition of *The Modern Corporation* have continued: the concentration of economic power, the dispersion of ownership, and the separation of ownership and control" (Berle and Means 1968, p. 359; see also pp. xxix, xxx). The "concentration of economic power represented by the share of the national wealth and income in the hands of the major corporations and the trend in these shares" was one of the circumstances which continued to motivate and channel Means's analysis of inflation until his death (Ware, foreword to Means 1988, p. 1).[9]

The implication of these trends, in Means's view, continued to be that identified in 1932, namely, that "it is now necessary to think, to a very important extent, in terms of these huge units rather than in terms of the multitude of small competing elements of private enterprise. The emphasis must be shifted to that very great proportion of industry in the hands of a relatively few units, units which can be studied individually and concretely" and therefore to "a society in which production governed by blind economic forces is being replaced by one in which production is carried on under the ultimate control of a handful of individuals" (Berle and Means 1932, pp. 45, 46). The growth of the corporation, of corporate giants, and of the concentration of economic power in a relatively few corporations—

as well as the dispersion of stock ownership and the separation of ownership and control—inexorably raises the question of the accountability of corporations and their management. This growth also raises questions of the relation of the corporation, and corporate system, to the market and to government, further emphasizing the political significance of positive analysis.

Means pioneered the use of industry concentration ratios.[10] That their status remains controversial is due to at least two factors, both involving selective perception: first, absent an agreed-upon base representing nonconcentration, ambiguity exists regarding their numerical significance; and second, there are fundamental conceptual controversies over the relationship between structural and behavioral, or process, aspects of competition and concerning their relative significance. Means did not deny the relevance of the behavioral or process aspects, but he did believe that rivalrous competition was different from traditional notions of pure, or Smithian, atomistic competition, and that the consequences for the performance of the economy due to these differences were important and should be studied. Means never ceased to question the belief that competition was "an effective regulator of profits where the great modern corporations are concerned," as assumed by "traditional profit theory" (Means 1933, pp. 174, 175). The performance consequences which he had in mind included allocative ones, but also and most especially macroeconomic income- and inflation-determining ones.

4. Dispersion of Stock Ownership

One of Means's critical empirical findings pertaining to the modern corporation was the dispersion of stock ownership. This was the thesis of his first solely authored article (Means 1930), included in his accepted dissertation, and of chapter 4 of *The Modern Corporation and Private Property*. The post–World War II growth of stock ownership aided this dispersion, notwithstanding the growth of pension and mutual funds, etc. (Berle and Means 1968, pp.

343ff.). For Means, the increasing dispersion of stock ownership both grew out of and made possible, that is, emanated from and reinforced, the concentration of economic power in the modern corporation (Berle and Means 1932, p. 47).

Means, along with Berle, stressed certain implications of the rise of the corporation accompanied by this dispersion of ownership. The picture portrayed by these implications represented to them no small part of the transformation of the economy. Those who identified capitalism in terms characteristic of the corporation, as if those terms were generic to the system *qua* system, failed to appreciate the enormity of the transformation both in terms of structure and the ordinary life of people. As enumerated at the end of their chapter on dispersion of stock ownership (Berle and Means 1932, pp. 66–68), these implications are:

1. Most fundamental of all, the position of ownership has changed from that of an active to that of a passive agent. . . .
2. The spiritual values that formerly went with ownership have been separated from it. . . .
3. The value of an individual's wealth is coming to depend on forces entirely outside himself and his own efforts. . . .
4. The value of the individual's wealth not only fluctuates constantly—the same may be said of most wealth—but it is subject to a constant appraisal. . . .
5. Individual wealth has become extremely liquid through the organized markets. . . .
6. Wealth is less and less in a form which can be employed directly by its owner. . . .
7. Finally, in the corporate system, the "owner" of industrial wealth is left with a mere symbol of ownership while the power, the responsibility and the substance which have been an integral part of ownership in the past are being transferred to a separate group in whose hands lies control.

These features of modern life comprise most of the fundamental elements which Means and Berle believed to have constituted the revolution in economic organization wrought by the corporation.

5. Separation of Ownership and Control

As just noted, the separation of ownership and control was a principal accompaniment to the corporate revolution. It, too, for Means was both a cause and a consequence of the growth of the corporation and the corporate system. In particular, it was a consequence of the dispersion of stock ownership which itself was both cause and (perhaps especially) consequence of the rise of organized stock exchanges.

It is not too much to say that the thesis of the separation of ownership and control became to many the central message of *The Modern Corporation and Private Property*. In our view, however, the separation thesis is but one—albeit important—theme of the book. Also to be stressed are the transformation of the nature of private property (which is true even if the separation thesis is rejected and, therefore, the dispersion thesis finessed), the concentration of corporate power, and, indeed, the rise of the corporation and the corporate system itself. Several aspects of the separation thesis require attention: the meaning of control, the significance of profit maximization, and the matter of separation per se.

(a) The Meaning of Control

Prior to and during the early years of the modern corporation a small group of owners participated in corporate decision making and the exercise of discretion in the acquisition, use, and disposition of corporate assets. These owners were the corporation, quite aside from the eventually predominant legal fiction of corporate personhood (Samuels and Miller 1987). The self-identity of the corporation was determined by them. What constituted profit seeking, if not profit making and profit maximizing, were determined by them. All this changed with the development of the modern corporation.

As Berle and Means put it, the new system tended to "develop a division of the functions formerly accorded to ownership," and this "calls for an examination of the exact nature of these functions; the interrelation of the groups performing them; and the new position which these groups hold in the community at large" (1932, p. 119).

Although we cannot examine the (complex and confusing if not confused) historical detail here, Means's writings exhibit a rather complex and kaleidoscopic understanding of the meaning of "control," the concept from *The Modern Corporation and Private Property* which has been the object of the most critical attention. Means early insisted on the need to distinguish between ownership, management, and control. In this latter case, control signified the relatively small group of owners (perhaps the original promoters or their successors) who exercised de facto ultimate discretion over corporate affairs. It was they who chose, instructed, and oversaw the management; it was they "who had the power to select the directors" (Lee 1988c, p. 15). The other stockholders were passive, more or less along for whatever ride they came to enjoy. This understanding, it seems, reflected Means's observations and studies of the corporation during the period of finance capitalism, especially the practices of the great financiers and the great industrial moguls, including the economic wars for control between factions or between insiders and outsiders (what in the 1980s came to be called hostile takeovers by corporate raiders). In these cases, or the genre which they represented, control meant to Means the faction with effective exercise of discretion in contrast to the losers and/or the passive stockholders whose only connection to the corporation was to have purchased its securities on the open market rather than to have been a vital part of its operation. (See Lee 1988b, pp. 9ff., 22.[11])

Eventually, while not discrediting the significance of factional control, Means seems to have recognized that the underlying phenomenon was not merely or not necessarily the distinction between control in the hands of all stockholders and control in the hands of a faction, whether minority or majority (but generally the former). The more general and fundamental phenomenon was the unbundling of the functions of ownership—capital supply, goal formation, operational decision making, and profit receipt.[12] Stockholding now basically meant the passive receipt of dividends in return for having either originally supplied corporate capital or subsequently purchasing the securities of those who had, whereas the other functions—goal formation and operational decision making (for example, determining precisely and strategically what profit seeking and maximizing are to mean for the company; decision making over funds, or assets)—were now located elsewhere.

What this "elsewhere" could be was complex. It could, as contemplated earlier, be an ownership faction. It could be a self-perpetuating board of directors *cum* upper management and/or the entire management (though with different degrees of participation in decision making). Or it could be what John Kenneth Galbraith (1967) was eventually to call the technostructure, with some or many decision-making details necessarily made deep below the board of directors, though subject to its review—perhaps in conjunction with a distinctive ownership faction but perhaps not. It could be, in whole or in part, in the hands of external financial institutions: investment bankers, commercial banks, insurance companies, or pension funds, either through stockholding per se (perhaps effectively constituting factions) or through borrowing relationships. The crux was not the role of a narrow notion of factional control but separation of ownership *qua* ownership from the strategic and operational decision making which comprised the daily affairs of the corporation.

An alternative way of looking at this is to define de facto property ownership as the capacity to make decisions about the acquisition, deployment, and disposal of assets, including the division of profits between retained earnings and dividends. In this view, ownership must effectually be said to be lodged in the total managerial structure of the corporation, including but not limited to the board of directors. The de jure owners, the stockholders, are generally merely passive, contingent recipients of dividends hoping also for market appreciation based on the effective use and capitalization of retained earnings (as well as favorable stock market conditions). In this way, ownership is control, but not defined to reside with the stockholders; de facto ownership is where the actual decision-making power resides. But this linguistic usage was not that followed by either Means or the literature dealing with control. Ownership was defined, rather, in terms of the ownership of equity securities, and one then sought to identify the locus of decision making, or control.

The crux, then, of the doctrine of the separation of ownership and control is that effective decision making is placed in the hands of persons other than those who hold a majority of the ownership rights (that is, equity securities) (paraphrasing Ware, foreword to Means 1988, p. 1). Indeed, control can rest in a management (including the board of directors) with members who do not own equity securities. Ownership as ownership of securities is different from ownership as decision making, or control. Moving up the corporate ladder typically has more meaning so far as participating in corporate decision making than does the acquisition of additional equity securities, certainly for the great majority of stockholders.

The world is that of the managerial corporation. "The shareowners as owners are legally responsible for the management of their business firms,[13] yet the non-owning managements have the actual powers of control" (Bain 1968, p. 74). The idea of the separation of ownership from decision making, or control in that sense if not also in regard to a controlling ownership faction, was not original with Berle and Means. The idea had a considerable earlier history; indeed, as Lee (1988b, p. 19) notes, "the topic itself had long been a favorite of Progressives because of the unsavory implications it had for the large corporation." This latter concern reflects the perceived cultural and moral significance of the changed nature of the economic organization of the economy consequent to the rise of the modern corporation and its changed organization of corporate control. Whatever one's views on the matter, the question of control had been perceived and debated before Berle and Means wrote on it. But it was then, as now, a critical feature of the economic organization of modern economic society, whatever moral and cultural evaluation is given the putative structural changes which have taken place in it.

(b) Profit Maximization

At issue, almost from the very beginning, was the nature of the consequences of the structural changes in the relationship between ownership and control which have accrued in modern economic society. Many writers have accepted the separation of ownership and control (in the sense of decision making, as used hereafter) but have questioned, if not denied, its significance because, arguably, management and equity security owners have the same objective, namely, profit maximization. Even when control is viewed as factional control, the gain of the faction is seen as leading to the gain of the other stockholders. In an alternative formulation, there is a market for control which serves to protect the profit-maximizing interests of the otherwise passive stockholders. There are several important and subtle issues here.

Profit maximization is a formal, substantively empty term. Profit maximization is both subjective and problematic. There is no independent test of (1) whether a corporate decision or decisional strategy is in fact profit maximizing and (2) whether actually registered profits are in fact the maximum that could have been earned given all conditions.

We have, of course, the authority of Coase (1988, p. 19) that economic formalism presented on the blackboard does not at all represent what transpires in the corporation. The ordinary daily life of corporations is taken up not only with the making and execution of policy, but with determining what constitutes the very substance of profit maximization. It is one thing to formally portray profit maximization as the equalization of marginal revenue and marginal cost, or the maximization of the spread between total revenue and total cost, or as the making of marginalist revenue versus cost decisions along a multiplicity of margins. It is quite another to learn and make judgments about alternative products, technologies, production functions, markets, marketing strategies, financing strategies, techniques for identifying opportunities and assessing them, and techniques of implementation in each of these areas, and so on. It is never obvious what decisions will be effective in pursuit of greater, let alone maximum, profits. For many economists, perhaps especially those most critical of Means's argument, profit maximization is a black box, a formal category. Means's argument is not understood unless one appreciates that corporate decision making is infinitely more complex than simply profit maximization. What is important is not merely profit maximization (even accepting that as a meaningful objective function for the firm), but determining the directions and further operational details of the substance of profit maximization.

We also seem to know three things concerning the relationship between ownership and control on the one hand and profit maximization on the other: (1) Members of corporate management disagree as to the details of what constitutes profit maximization, and much of the time, effort and productive imagination of management is taken up with the attempt to work out those conflicts of detail which, given market conditions, will govern realized profits. (2) Most stockholders are fundamentally ignorant of the complex details of running "their" company, this notwithstanding the often greater sophistication of specialists in security brokerage firms and large investment institutions. (3) Stockholders are not homogeneous of view and also likely would differ among themselves as to what constitutes for them the desirable putative profit-maximizing strategy.

It is simply an assumption that managerial profit maximization (assuming that that is what they are undertaking) is the same thing as stockholder profit maximization. What is the desirable amount of leverage, the desirable debt-equity ratio, and many similar questions, have answers which, as between management and equity stockholders, and among the latter, are likely to differ significantly. It is both possible and likely that the interests of equity owners will diverge from each other and from the interests of management (control).

Berle and Means were also, and to some extent especially, attentive to the opportunities open to management (or control) to conduct corporate affairs in such a manner as to benefit themselves in contrast to, and to the putative detriment of, the equity owners. One could view the division between retained earnings and dividends as, so far as decision-making control is concerned, a distribution between management (seeking greater assets to manage—empire, opportunities) and equity owners (who no longer have direct control over "their" profits). To affirm that equity owners benefit through prospective appreciation via capitalization of profits generated by retained earnings, if only through capital acquisition at lowest cost, is but an assumption. To argue that dissident stockholders can vote with their feet is only to say that they can buy securities in other corporations in which management makes similar decisions.

Several points support the view that the interests of management and stockholders may diverge. First, there is the historic capacity of management to engage in personally beneficial quid pro quo contracts, if not also sweetheart contracts, with other firms, including firms separately owned by management, that is of "pursuing a policy of personal enrichment to the detriment of the owners" (Lee 1988c, p. 16). Second, management has historically had the capacity to establish its own financial arrangements in a manner favorable to its members, including "executive bonuses or discretionary additions to their salaries, the cost of special perquisites to managers, expenditures on administrative staff" (Bain 1968, p. 73), and so on. Third, financial and securities markets have only limited power to counter widespread practices inimical to equity owners. Fourth, there are differences in the information available to management and to equity owners, and among equity owners, and hence consequential differences in objective function that are likely to ensue.

The significance of these and other points depends in part upon one's perception of both how the corporate system operates and how it should operate, and of any difference between the two. Something of how much the system of economic organization has changed and of how different it could be, is given by Hayek's (1967, pp. 300ff.) proposals that, first, stockholders individually have the right to determine the distribution of profits between dividends and retained earnings and, second, that voting rights accompanying corporate ownership of stock in another corporation be eliminated. For Hayek, such institutional changes would create a greater and more competitive market for capital. In this view it is altogether possible for the interests of management (control) and equity owners to diverge. Unless the latter are allowed to have and the former are forced to have access to the capital market, the economy has a very different performance than it otherwise would.[14] Hayek believes that performance under his proposed arrangements would be superior because the allocative decisions would be made by the equity owners, not management. This view presumes at least three things: first, that management has substantial discretion in both pursuing profit maximization and distributing profits; second, that profit maximization need not be identical either between management and equity owners or among equity owners; and third, that analysts necessarily make some assumption as to the superiority of one arrangement over the other.

There is a strong tendency, understandable under the aegis of neoclassical economics, to evaluate the managerial-control thesis by comparison of profit rates between management- and owner-controlled firms. It is not clear that this test is a test of anything significant. It appears at first glimpse that if institutional structures were significantly different, the difference would be reflected in differential profit rates. But that is not the point. Profit rates do not reflect what goes on within the corporation as regards the relations between management and stockholders or between factional control and all other owners. In particular, profit rates do not get at the larger questions recited by Berle in his introduction to the first edition of *The Modern Corporation and Private Property* (Berle and Means 1932, pp. vii–viii) and quoted as part of the epigraph to the first chapter in Means's draft dissertation:

> The translation of perhaps two-thirds of the industrial wealth of the country from individual ownership to ownership by the large, publicly financed corporations vitally changes the lives of property owners, the lives of workers, and the methods of property tenure. The divorce of ownership from control consequent on that process almost necessarily involves a new form of economic organization of society. (Means 1933, p. 2)

The price-profit, marginal adjustment paradigm of neoclassical economics, for all its admitted areas of strength, is simply not capable of meaningfully penetrating these larger questions. There is more to the world of the corporation than equalized versus unequalized profit rates.

It was Means's view that equity owners might disagree among themselves as to desired corporate goals. To say that dissident stockholders could always sell their interests underscores his point that for most stockholders all that was involved was ownership of securities and not participation in management-control. Moreover, the personal interests of management may well differ from those of stockholders. Management may have more interest in general corporate stability and growth, as a framework within which to pursue managerial careers, or it may be excessively preoccupied with achieving short-term goals as prerequisite to promotions; and equity owners may seek either stable long-term growth or quick profits. There is, in Means's view, no internal way in which equity owners can exercise an effective voice. Exit is hardly participation. In any event, corporations, in Means's view, did not price their products to maximize profits by responding to and taking advantage of every variation in market forces, preferring, it seems, to price with longer-period and general corporate planning purposes in mind. The crux is the process by which "profit maximization" comes to have substantive meaning and is pursued and administered within the corporation.

It seems apparent, then, that the separation of ownership and management (control) is historically what has occurred and that arguments concerning the irrelevance of this separation to profit maximization are essentially empty and presumptive.[15]

There is, finally, the question of the justification by which stockowner returns are deemed legitimate. This is *not* a question which Means posed in order to argue for fundamental changes in institutions, for example, to emasculate passive stockowners. Means, like Berle (for example, in his preface to Berle and Means 1968, pp. xxiv–xxv), called attention to the question of legitimacy insofar as it depended upon power relations grounded upon (for example) the law of the corporation, to emphasize the need to consider the ramifications of the corporate revolution. Berle and Means were conservative men, but they were candid men, believing that policy ought to be made on the basis of informed judgment, not assumption guided by myth and ideology. Specifically, their interpretation of the modern economic system, after the corporate revolution, raised the question posed by Means in the unaccepted draft of his dissertation, "whether the striving for industrial profits can any longer be treated as a satisfactory incentive to action in the conduct of industry" (Means 1933, p. 3a). Similarly, Means pointed out in his thesis summary "that if the logic of traditional profit theory were to be followed, any profits over and above enough given to the 'owners' to induce the continued supply of new capital should be received by control as a prize to induce the efficient management of enterprise." He thus raised the question "whether profits are a socially effective method of inducing enterprise activity [where the modern corporation is concerned]" (Means 1962a, p. 19, bracketed phrase in published but not original version).[16]

(c) The Separation of Ownership and Control

The question of the separation of ownership and control (management) is extremely complex and kaleidoscopic. That common stock ownership is not control in the historic sense is unequivocally true.

Ownership and control are separate in the modern corporation. The modern corporation is controlled by a group, nominally hired agents or managers, other than the body of stockholders as a whole. Those in control are able to make decisions which are in their own interest, or what they understand to be the interest of the corporation, rather than being bound by the interests of the body of stockholders as a whole. That the two sets of interests are homogeneous or identical is an assumption. The fact is that managements are decision makers; stockholders, decision takers. Whether takeover conflicts between rival factions, factions perhaps quite new to stock ownership, constitute an effective blurring of the distinction or only something analogous to rivalry between cliques within the managerial class, is a matter of subjective perception.

Managerial discretion models, such as Williamson's (1967), recognize that discretion is not unconstrained but, consistent with the separation of ownership and control thesis, affirm, as one textbook puts it, "that managers can pursue their own self-interest once they have achieved the goals of keeping profits at an acceptable level, paying sufficient dividends to the stockholders, and causing the firm to grow" (Koch 1974, p. 39). The crux of the matter, of course, is what governs stockholder expectations (which are heavily influenced both by past managerial decisions and managerial pronouncements of what corporate survival and success requires—not just within one major corporation but similarly among all or most of them). In any case, the great majority of stockownership interests are without control. "It is control and not the owners who have become the driving power behind modern enterprise" (Means 1933, p. 172).

There are numerous other considerations. For example, one must consider what Taussig (1930, pp. 92–94) called the "instinct of domination," "not merely money-making in itself . . . [but to] no small degree, . . . the instinct to suffer no opposition to control." Taussig noted that this explained the attitude and behavior of employers to unions: "The strong employer's desire to crush the union is not merely the outcome of cold calculations of profit;

unaware of what is working within him, he obeys a primal impulse."

The same applies to historic managerial attitudes toward stockholdership, notwithstanding the usual exercises of corporate rhetoric, including the lip service given the theory that the management and all other employees are working for the stockholders. For the history of the law of stockholder-management relations has been one of the progressive reduction of the rights of equity owners and the progressive enhancement of the decision-making authority of management coupled with the latter's insulation from dissident stockholders. Indeed, one of the things which Berle and Means (1932, Book II) traced was the historic regrouping of rights and the changed position of ownership and control.

As Commons (1950, p. 317) expressed the matter, protections originally established for the protection of stockholders "were relaxed, nearly always in the direction of greater power for the management and less protection for the individual shareholder, though apparently justified in the interest of the shareholders." The doctrine of implied consent and the practice of attributed, that is, assumed, identity of interests, masked a great many changes of relative power through the changing of corporation laws. As Commons also put it, "Berle and Means describe this evolution of corporation law in America . . . permitting the management to become supreme through reducing the rights of stockholders" (p. 318). Centralization of power in management provided "that unity of central management required to meet the competition of those [corporations] which had centered authority in the management" (p. 319). But while this view of the justification for the ongoing changes points to the selection process inherent in power play, it does not negate the fact that management and stockholder interests could diverge. While changes in relative management-shareholder rights (which seemingly disempowered equity owners) could possibly be in their interest, the intensity of managerial resolve to suffer no opposition—and the conflicts over these changes in the law of corporations—seem to call into question, if not belie, the assumption that shareowner and management interests necessarily coincide (or coincide sufficiently to warrant the assumption that they do).

Commons also quotes the investment adviser, Roger Babson, who may still stand as a suggestive critic of the existing system. Babson is quoted as saying in a 1938 speech that

> the average small stockholder is too often misled. He puts his money into the securities of companies about which he knows little or nothing. The information he receives is too often vague, incomplete and meaningless. Decisions are concentrated in the hands of an inside group of officials, bankers and lawyers. . . . Few of these directors would handle their own money as they have handled their stockholders' funds. (Commons 1950, p. 322)

And,

> Small stockholders need a union. . . . To watch over their own interests, therefore, investors need a protective organization just as workers need unions and political parties need machines.

The point is not whether Babson was correct, but that the assumption that the profit-maximizing interests of management (control) and stockholders coincide is highly subjective, ideological, and problematic, and subject to no independent test.

It is perfectly true that dissident stockholders have recourse to the security markets and that management must accommodate stockowner or potential stockowner interests and preferences sufficiently to attract and retain capital.[17] It is also arguable that the intensive interests of certain investors, such as mutual funds, pension funds, and other institutional investors, can serve as an effective check on the power of management in the interest of all stockholders. In addition, to the extent that management has direct or contingent interests in equity ownership (for example, through stock option plans at favorable prices), they have an interest in maximizing the capitalized value of profits, at least insofar as equity security prices do this. It is also true, for example, that, as Commons (1950, p. 324) pointed out, "the economic power of management over investors and the public generally differs greatly at different times." Yet these factors do not unambiguously point to an identity of interests, even within existing institutional arrangements. Moreover, the relationship between stockholders' interests and those of management would be quite different under, for example, Hayek's proposed alternative institutional arrangements, thus calling into question the presumptive identity of managerial and stockholder interests.

The identity of general managerial and stockholder interests and the claim that management and stockholders alike pursue corporate profit maximization are fundamentally assumptions and not subject to independent test. It is also the case that judgments about whether specific corporate policies are in the interests of stockholders are a matter of presumptive reasoning. Through such reasoning, anything that management decides to carry out can be said—assumed—to be in the interest of stockholder profits because otherwise management would not have made that decision.

All this is not to say that the present arrangements cannot work, for they obviously do. Nor does it mean that management and equity-owner interests need diverge to such an extent as to become an issue: radically asymmetrical information and general stockholder passivity, including the mesmerization of stockholders by existing management in a manner akin to political propaganda, work to the opposite effect. But it does point to the fundamentally changed structure of the economic organization of the economy and the consequences of this new structure. The identification of the changed structure and its consequences was, after all, the chief objective of *The Modern Corporation and Private Property* and much of Berle's and almost all of Means's subsequent work. Managerial discretion is important. One is tempted to follow the rhetorical lead of some monetarists to affirm that managerial discretion matters, indeed, matters most, without affirming that it is absolute.[18]

It is not surprising, therefore, that discussions of the corporation sometimes take on a theological trapping,[19] for the presence and exercise of corporate power raises questions of a moral nature. But the point of principal relevance here is that structural considerations severely limit the force of justification by reference to the "market." Markets are structured by, and give effect to, the institutional power structure which produces and operates through them—including corporations and the markets which they help form. Arguments about how solutions to problems relevant to the several parties to the corporation are worked out through markets cannot claim uniqueness and conclusiveness because they are worked out through markets. This is because what is worked out through markets is specific to the institutional or power structure which forms and works through the market; that is, there is no unique Pareto-optimal solution to such problems.

Considerations of propriety and efficacy raise the kind of concern originally posed in England in the 1790s and in the United States in the 1840s, in debate over both corporations per se and general incorporation laws. The possibility that hired managers, lacking incentive, would not necessarily have the same diligence as owners, now so much resolved by assumption, and such other questions as why moral investors would desire to limit their liability, now so largely taken for granted, were then quite commonly raised, suggesting that the questions of the separation of ownership and management (control) and its cultural and institutional integument were present from the very inception of the modern institution of the corporation.

Indeed, doubts about the joint stock company, the precursor of the modern corporation, are stressed in Adam Smith's *Wealth of Nations*. Smith wrote, for example, that the proprietors who control management "seldom pretend to understand any thing of the business of the company; and when the spirit of faction happens not to prevail among them, give themselves no trouble about it, but receive contentedly such half yearly or yearly dividend, as the directors think proper to make to them.'' Moreover,

> the directors of such companies, however, being the managers rather of other people's money than of their own, it cannot well be expected, that they should watch over it with the same anxious vigilance with which the partners in a private co-partnery frequently watch over their own. Like the stewards of a rich man, they are apt to consider attention to small matters as not for their master's honour, and very easily give themselves a dispensation from having it. Negligence and profusion, therefore, must always prevail, more or less, in the management of the affairs of such a company. It is upon this account that joint stock companies for foreign trade have seldom been able to maintain the competition against private competitors. They have, accordingly, very seldom succeeded without an exclusive privilege; and frequently have not succeeded with one. Without an exclusive privilege they have commonly mismanaged the trade. With an exclusive privilege they have both mismanaged and confined it. (Smith 1937, pp. 699, 700)[20]

Means also insisted that, as twin bases for the great size of the predominant modern corporations, there had been two developments. The first was the Industrial Revolution, the second, the Corporate Revolution, and it was deemed important by him that ''the key development in each case has been essentially the same, namely, a separation of the control over one of the factors of production from the possessor of that factor.'' The Industrial Revolution, with the factory system, ''brought an increasingly large number of workers directly under a single management. This meant that the workers during working hours surrendered control over their activity to a large extent to a central management over whom they had little control. This in turn meant that production instead of being organized through the interaction of independent individuals trading in the market, could in part be organized on a planned basis.'' Prior to ''the development of corporate enterprises, a limit was set to the size of enterprise by the wealth of the individual owner. . . . [and] his immediate associates.'' But ''through the Modern Corporation, the separation of ownership and control has broken down this barrier to further extension in the size of enterprise (or has resulted from the breaking down of this barrier to size) and the area which can be operated as a coordinated whole has been extended. In this case it is the possessor of wealth rather than the worker who has surrendered control to the unified management. As a result, just as the status of the worker was radically altered when he shifted his position from independent owner-worker to wage worker, so the status of the owner has been radically altered by his surrender of control'' (Means 1933, pp. 5–6; see also Means in Berle and Means 1968, p. xxx).

But there is more. The modern corporation is perhaps above all an institution for the accumulation of capital (which is not to say that all corporations perform that function). Central to every modern economic system is its process for the accumulation of capital. Historically, in capitalist market economies the saving-investment process has been tied to the concentration of income in upper income brackets. This remains the case but is now more complex. One factor is the growth of large-scale depository and nondepository financial institutions, especially pension funds, mutual funds, and insurance companies, which are principal means by which the savings of masses of people are collected in a centralized, nongovernmental manner. But the giant corporation, financing much of its investment through retained earnings and only partly dependent on organized capital markets, is to no small degree independent from individual saving and capital markets (Berle in Berle and Means 1968, p. xxv). ''Management thus becomes, in an odd sort of way, the uncontrolled administrator of a kind of trust having the privilege of perpetual accumulation. The stockholder is the passive beneficiary, not only of the original 'trust,' but of the compounded annual accretions to it'' (Berle in Berle and Means 1968, p. xv).

6. The Corporate System: The Economy as a System of Power

John Maynard Keynes wrote in 1926 (p. 52) of the "tendency of big enterprise to socialize itself" through the dissociation of stockholders from the management of corporations. This had been preceded by well-known arguments by Werner Sombart and Thorstein Veblen as to the transformation of capitalism from the stage of entrepreneurial heroics to that of routinist administration. It was followed by James Burnham's (1941) argument that in all areas of modern life, but especially the economic, a revolution had been progressing in which a new elite of administrative managers was replacing traditional leaders, for example, the capitalist entrepreneur. And then came Schumpeter.

Ten years after the publication of *The Modern Corporation and Private Property*, Joseph Alois Schumpeter, in *Capitalism, Socialism and Democracy* (1942), argued that individualist entrepreneurial capitalism was being replaced by what he called socialist civilization. But, as one of the present authors has argued elsewhere (Samuels 1985, pp. 89ff.), the reality which Schumpeter describes as the new stage is at least in part the growth of the corporation, especially the giant corporation, and the corporate bureaucratization and routinization of the entrepreneurial function. "The modern corporation, it is his [Schumpeter's] central thesis, socialized the bourgeois mind and property as well as business risk. It ousts the bourgeoisie (or the entrepreneurs in their midst) from the function to which they have owed their social weight. Business is increasingly controlled by a small number of bureaucratized corporations in which progress is mechanized and planned" (p. 90). As Schumpeter himself expressed the matter (1928, pp. 385–386, quoted in Samuels 1985, p. 117, note 141), capitalism itself has created "an order of things which it will be merely matter of taste and terminology to call Socialism or not."

These writers, with markedly different world views, all antedated Galbraith's *New Industrial State* (1967). Galbraith pictured a system of private-public planning in the center of which is the corporation and its technostructure to which "power in the business enterprise and power in the society has passed" (p. 60), all "adapted to the needs of advanced technology and the large amounts of capital and comprehensive planning which this requires" (p. 86).

Though Berle and Means's analyses detailed "the growing dominance of the corporate form, the increasing decision-making power of corporate management, the increasingly passive position of shareholders, and the increasing inapplicability of the ethical and economic justifications given (rightly enough at the time) by classic economics" (Berle in Berle and Means 1968, p. viii), their argument went beyond the corporation per se. They emphasized the "massive collectivization of property devoted to production, with accompanying decline of individual decision-making and control" (p. xxv), in short, "the trend toward dominance of that collective capitalism we call the 'corporate system' . . . ," a trend which in 1968 "continued unabated" (p. viii).

The concept of the "corporate system" is certainly not unambiguous.[21] But it is no less ambiguous than such historically used terms as "individualism," "collectivism," "capitalism," "socialism," and "free enterprise." Perhaps the most widespread conceptual apparatus absorbed by people acculturated in Western civilization (and increasingly elsewhere) is the distinction between "private" and "public." These concepts at best are interdependent and in practice are subject to ubiquitous selective perception and attribution of content. Private rights, for example, are universally considered private whereas their precise form and economic significance is a function of the public legal and statutory processes, which in turn have significant nominally private inputs. The idea of the corporation has a complex linguistic and ideological history, but it is no exaggeration to note that it became transformed from a public to a private concept during the nineteenth century (Samuels and Miller 1987, for example, chapters 2, 3, 6, and 7, and pp. 119–120). The transformation from individual enterprise to corporate enterprise, or from personal to collective enterprise, was accompanied by relatively little change in the semantics of the dominant ideology. Giant corporations are treated the same as the sole proprietorship by both ideology and, for most purposes, mainstream economics. Commons (1950, p. 298), on the other hand, interpreted Berle and Means as having identified a new form of economic system in which "organized and maneuvered collective action in control of individual action" predominates.

Means insisted that the predominance of the corporation meant that the entire economic system had been fundamentally transformed—its structure, its microeconomics, its macroeconomics, and its processes of economic adjustment had changed.

One aspect of the corporate system is indicated by what Means called the "corporate community." As Lee (1988a, pp. 33–34) summarizes the matter,

> through interlocking directorates, intercorporate minority stockholders, the activities of the larger financial corporations in the use which they make of their investment funds at their disposal, and the interrelationships resulting from the servicing of the large corporations, there existed, he argued, a corporate community in which corporate managers reside. Moreover, within the corporate community there also existed corporate interest groupings which consisted of a core corporate institution(s) and a number of satellite corporate enterprises. As a result of these community relationships, Means felt that "the controls exercised by this corporate community among the larger corporations are of major importance." (Quoting Means 1939, p. 163)

Means also wrote that

> many of the individuals making up this corporate community also hold responsible positions in medium-sized and smaller corporations. The larger banks can exercise some influence over smaller banks through the system of banking correspondents and over smaller companies through the loan of funds. The larger corporations are often in a position to influence the managements of enterprises from which they purchase their raw material or to which they sell their products. The nonmarket controls exercised by the corporate community thus extend

> beyond the larger corporations. The main importance of the corporate community, however, lies in the controls exercised over the policies of the larger corporations, through them affecting the whole American economy. (Means 1939, p. 163, quoted in Lee 1988a, p. 56, note 38)

In short, what Lindblom (1977) calls "the privileged position of business" in the United States is most distinctively, though by no means completely, that of large corporate business.

Means did not claim that the economy consisted solely of the corporate system. Most fundamental is Means's view that the modern economy is a *dual* economy, comprised of an essentially competitive, largely but not completely individual enterprise sector, and an essentially oligopolistic, privately planned core. In other words, in addition to informal rules or customs (double-entry bookkeeping and the pace of work in the shop) and socially approved goals (profit making and other indicia of success), Means emphasized two mechanisms of coordination: the market and corporate administration. As we shall see, the Coasian theory of the firm substantially presumes Means's understanding. And as we shall also see, the fact of this dual economy has significant implications for the microfoundations, operation, and performance of the macroeconomy.

Perhaps the most suggestive support for the Berle and Means thesis of the rise of the corporate system and the ascendance of managerial administration, has been the development of a managerialist ideology. The traditional individualist ideology has interpreted the corporation along more or less traditional individualist lines as just another individual economic actor not very different from the sole proprietorship, especially in being subject to the overriding forces of the market. The newer managerialist ideology affirms the corporation and its managers as having power not totally circumscribed by the market, power utilized to perform important managerial (read: allocative and distributional) functions in conjunction with if not in place of the market. (See Samuels and Miller 1987, pp. 120–122 and the citations given on p. 128, note 19.) More recent ideological developments seem to have returned to the individualist ideology in which the corporation's power is obscured by defining it as a single person subject to the market understood to be *ipso facto* competitive. Ironically, the last century has seen the elevation of the doctrine of corporate personhood (and thus the encapsulation into law of the individualist ideology) contemporaneous with the rise of the corporate system (Samuels and Miller 1987, p. 121).

The individualist ideology cannot fully obfuscate, however, the predominance of standardized contracts. These are typically drawn up by the seller (but in transactions among business firms—for example, between larger manufacturers and the multiplicity of their suppliers—often by the buyer), which consumers can only accept or reject, that is, they can take it or leave it. Absent is the bargaining supposedly generic to free contract contemplated by traditional capitalist ideology and traditional economic theory (except for its mechanistic Walrasian formulation, which has no room even for that). As Means saw the matter, this is not a question of immorality but is required by a technologically advanced, highly organized corporate system, which must be recognized—with its administered, standardized contracts—for what it is in both theory and policy.

7. The Changing Meaning of Private Property: Collectivized

Much of the interpretive and critical literature generated by *The Modern Corporation and Private Property* has focused, not improperly, on the thesis of the separation of ownership and control. Much of Means's later work dealt with the prevalence of administered prices and its micro- and macroeconomic consequences, especially in regard to inflation, and, again not improperly, much of the interpretive and critical literature has dealt with it. But one cannot read or understand the work of Berle and Means without appreciating the significance of the private property in the title of their classic work. For their argument is that the rise of the corporation and the corporate system has meant a fundamental transformation of the substance of private property. The significance of the thesis of the separation of ownership and control far transcends any statistical debate about relative rate of profits (between owner- and management-controlled firms) and any presumption as to the identity of interests between owners and managers. The crux is the rise of a species of property in which ownership is passive and, however dependent the economic significance of all property is on others through the market as well as on the law, directly dependent on decisions made by nominal agents.

This argument was heavily influenced by Berle, the lawyer and the senior author, but Means readily concurred. One can perceive the range and nuances of this transformation and of their emphasis on it, by examining the principal subheadings of their 1932 volume:

> Book I. Property in Flux: Separation of the attributes of ownership under the corporate system
>
> Book II. Regrouping of Rights: Relative legal position of ownership and control
>
> Book III. Property in the Stock Markets: Security exchanges as appraisers and liquidators
>
> Book IV. Reorientation of Enterprise: Effects of the corporate system on fundamental economic concepts

Moreover, included in Book IV, in addition to chapters on "The Traditional Logic of Profits," "The Inadequacy of Traditional Theory," and "The New Concept of the Corporation," is the first chapter, "The Traditional Logic of Property." Indeed, most impressive in the volume is the premier status given not to the separation of ownership and control per se, but to that of which it is both consequence and cause: the fundamental transformation of property—the leading institution of the capitalist market economy. "Must we not, therefore, recognize," Berle and Means (1932, p. 338) argued, "that we are no longer dealing with property in the old sense? Does the traditional logic of property still apply?" The growth of the corporation and the corporate system brought a transformation of the institution of private property no less significant than the replacement of feudal property by fee simple absolute, by the rise of private property itself.

The ensuing interpretive and policy question is not whether the rise of passive stockholding weakens the case for private property. The fact is, following Commons and Schumpeter, among others, that property has already been transformed from individual personal property to socialized or collectivized property. Its "private" versus "public" character is largely, though by no means entirely, semantic and ideological. The privateness which the old theory of individual personal property lauded is now used to represent and legitimize corporate property lacking the personal element of privateness. The representation of the corporation as a person is of course a legal fiction. The ultimate property foundation of the corporation is no longer individual personal property except in name only (Samuels and Miller 1987, pp. 121ff. and passim).

The function of the theory of property is not solely to interpret or explain but also to legitimize. Traditional property theory is now used to legitimize the corporation, its management, and, *mutatis mutandis*, the equity owners. The theory can be formulated either to include or to exclude government "regulation." The fundamental policy question is always channeled by selective interpretation or definition of reality. It concerns the status of the existing law of corporations: whether the law is to be left unchanged or there is to be a change in the law, or of the interests which law is used to support. Absent any policy objective to this volume, the point is that, in regard to equity owner rights, the changing nature of property has taken place both de facto and de jure and the theory of property must recognize both sources of change.

So far as interpretive description of reality is concerned, while far from calling for nationalization of already socialized or collectivized corporate property, Berle and Means say that government policy must recognize the changed nature of property. Certain interests are concerned with the maintenance of the older conception, hoping to forestall undesirable changes in government policy. As for economics, as Berle put the matter, "This wealth cannot be justified by the old economic maxims, despite passionate and sentimental arguments of neoclassic economists who would have us believe the old system has not changed." "Stockholders . . . are beneficiaries by position only. Justification for their inheritance must be sought outside classic economic reasoning" (Berle in Berle and Means 1968, pp. xxii, xxiii). Berle and Means are more interested in formulating a new theory of property, a new interpretive description of property, than in proposing revolutionary changes in policy. Indeed, so far as revolution is concerned, it is their principal, and conservative, point that the revolution in property has already taken place and must be accepted, not reversed.

The rise of the modern corporation was a principal facet of another major transformation of property, alongside and intertwined with that of passive versus active property. Property has become transformed from corporeal to incorporeal. Property is now (and, ironically, perhaps always had been in some ultimate sense) a bundle of expectations which have a market value and may bring income. It is neither physical assets nor an enterprise dominated by the property owner whose decisions govern the enterprise. Property, at least equity security property, is now known and valued for its liquidity and income-growth potential rather than for its decision-making authority (Berle and Means 1932, Book III).

Finally, the transformations described and interpreted by Berle and Means can be modeled in quite different ways. The changes in property rights can be traced to the existence of the modern corporation or the changes in the corporation can be traced to the changes in property rights. In both cases the critical factors, traced by Berle and Means in 1932, were the changes in the law—sometimes technically the law of property and other times the law of the corporation—such that the changes were both cumulative and simultaneous.

8. The Economy as a System of Power

Orthodox economic ideology and theory have portrayed the economy as a pacific, harmonious, and optimizing process which has the advantages, in part, of giving scope and effect to individual preferences and of generating remarkable growth in output. Berle and Means neither deny nor diminish the significance of this portrayal. Performance has some meaning in the limited sense of Pareto-optimality. But, they insist, the economy is above all a system of power and of power play. Emphasis on its putative characteristics of harmony and optimality is useful to the powerful and their intellectual allies in order to obfuscate the reality of power. Such emphasis must not obscure the power aspects of the economy, especially in regard to the modern corporation and the property system with which it is associated.

Berle and Means make several specific points, as we interpret them: (1) that what characterizes the system as much as if not more than its pacific, harmonious, and optimizing characteristics is power; (2) that not all individual preferences count equally; (3) that the structure of power (rights) weights preferences; and (4) that structural features of the economy—especially those centering on the modern corporation—have important performance consequences, most notably for macroeconomic stability. It is especially important to note that "power" is used here descriptively and analytically and not at all pejoratively. Power, to Means, was simply a fact of economic life, especially as it pertained to or was manifest in the corporation and the corporate system.

The significance of Gardiner Means in the history of economic thought rests to no small degree, then, on his status as a major interpreter of the economy as a system of power. This status in turn rests on his view of the corporation as an institution, of the corporate system, the dual economy, the separation of ownership and control, and the changing nature and meaning of private property, as well as of the importance of power for micro- and macroeconomic operation and performance, examined below. Power, as either participation per se or concentrated participation in economic decision making, transcends, for Means, industrial competition. Still, industry, in his view, is neither fully nor uniformly competitive. Individual economic entities are neither fully nor uniformly powerless. Rather, considerations of power, including but not limited to the structure of industry focusing on the modern corporation, are the dominant feature of the modern economy. Although Means's long-time focus on administered pricing has received the greatest attention by other economists, his view of the economy as a system of power is the most fundamental respect in which he did not conform to the belief system of the discipline. His emphasis on administered pricing itself is ultimately founded on that view.[22] Means thus insisted that economics was deficient insofar as it attributed to markets what was fundamentally and meaningfully a matter of power; indeed, the invocation of "market" was often, though by no means always, obscurantist.

One can readily interpret Means's lifetime research program as consisting of various inquiries into different aspects of the American economy as a system of power and its focal points of control. In his *Structure of the American Economy* (1939), the meaning of structure is rendered in part in terms of control and control in turn is understood in terms of power. Chapter 9, "The Structure of Controls," defines control as "the ability of one individual or group to influence the policies in respect to the use of resources which are adopted by another individual or group" (Means 1939, p. 153). Controls are distinguished as market and nonmarket, and various bases and structures of controls are identified. He examines "controls over the larger corporation"; management as "the center of policy formation"; "the corporate community," including interlocking directorates, intercorporate minority stockholders, interrelationships resulting from the servicing of the large corporations and from the control of investment funds, and corporate interest groupings; formal organizations representing economic interests; organizations based on business interests, including major business associations;[23] labor organizations; farmer organizations; consumer organizations; government, including government production, canalizing controls, industrial policies, and fiscal policies; and the "relation between government units and other elements in the control structure.''

In the institutionalist view of the economy it is not the market alone which organizes activity and allocates resources but the institutional and power structure which forms and operates through the market. Means is surely institutionalist in his conclusion as to ''the large extent to which the use of resources is not controlled by the market,'' and as to how the three sets of nonmarket controls, namely, ''the corporate community with its many ramifications and its climate of opinion; the major organizations representing the economic interests of business, labor, farmer, and consumer; and, finally, the Government units through which the conflicting interests of different economic groups are developed into a more or less effective working compromise[24] . . . combined with the market controls . . . appear to constitute the main essentials of the control structure'' (1939, pp. 169–170). Means understood the problem of the organization and control of the economy, with respect to which the concept of the economy as a system of power ultimately has meaning, and was able to transcend the saccharine implications of consumer sovereignty, however much the latter is also relevant. After all, the concept of Pareto-optimality totally ignores the structure within which exchange and the exhaustion of gains from trade take place. If the economy is a process of choice, it is also a structure and process of power or control—through which is determined whose choices count. It is a question of ''power and who makes what decisions'' (Means in Berle and Means 1968, p. xxxvii).

Instead of production ''being organized through the interaction of independent individuals trading in the market'' (Means 1933, p. 5; see Lee 1988a, p. 11), the surrender by workers and, eventually, stockholders of their control to a central management meant that production was to be organized in part on a planned basis. In such a situation, ideology and theory to the contrary notwithstanding, the structure and processes of power became important. In a comment on Hayek's description of a competitive economic system in *The Road to Serfdom*, Means wrote that

> if you introduce the power factor as a basic assumption into Hayek's competitive system, it takes on *an entirely new form* and many of his most important conclusions are seen to be faulty. This introduction of power relationships is as disrupting of the classical economic system as the assumption that a straight line is not the shortest distance between two points would be to Euclidean Geometry. (Means to William Benton, 26 December 1944. G. C. Means Papers, Series IV, Benton; quoted in Lee 1988a, pp. 36–37 note 1)

9. The Corporation as Private Government

In *The Modern Corporation and Private Property*, Berle and Means detailed, as summarized by Commons (1950, p. 307), the results of "the lawyers who advised the management and drafted the legislation which fitted the modern emergence of corporate management into the American scheme of economic and political government." This ongoing process is evidenced by the cultivation of the managerialist ideology, in which, for example, "The American corporation acts as a vital mediating structure between the powerful state and the individual" (Wolfson 1984, p. 151—a volume manifesting its obscurantist function through the subtitle: "Free Markets versus Regulation"). But notice what this means: The corporation is, as both Commons and Wolfson affirm, part of the total system of governance. The corporation is not merely a form by which production is organized. It is, along with "the family, the community organizations, churches and synagogues" (Wolfson 1984, p. 151) and the state (which to Wolfson is both ineffective and inefficient as well as largely undesirable), an institution of social control. In mediating between the state and the individual (as Wolfson puts it), the corporation is, in its decision making, also inexorably mediating between individuals, between individuals and groups of individuals, and between groups of individuals. It is a "private" government; it is "private" social control.

The corporation, in Means's view, also goes further. Insofar as the administrators of the corporation help determine the distribution of activity and decision making between corporate administration and the market (doing so, as Coase affirms, as rational economic persons), they are determining the structure of the system of governance in society and economy. Of what could private government consist more fundamentally than this?—especially in a world where corporations (and not bargaining) almost unilaterally determine standardized contracts of adhesion.

Corporate administration, again in Means's view, also constitutes private government in that it makes decisions with enormous concentrated consequences for the way of life and opportunities of others, decisions which, in contrast to the ordinary activities of single individuals in a Smithian economy, take on the quality of governance rather than of marginal adjustments to external stimuli, however much the latter are also involved.

The concluding paragraph of *The Modern Corporation and Private Property* (Berle and Means 1932, p. 357) contains a statement of the case for recognizing the corporation as private government in a system of economic power, which is as clear and concise as any:

> The rise of the modern corporation has brought a concentration of economic power which can compete on equal terms with the modern state—economic power versus political power, each strong in its own field. The state seeks in some aspects to regulate the corporation, while the corporation, steadily becoming more powerful, makes every effort to avoid such regulation. Where its own interests are concerned, it even attempts to dominate the state. The future may see the economic organism, now typified by the corporation, not only on an equal plane with the state, but possibly even superseding it as the dominant form of social organization. The law of corporations, accordingly, might well be considered as a potential constitutional law for the new economic state, while business practice is increasingly assuming the aspect of economic statesmanship.[25]

In 1988 these trends continue and, what is more, the nation-state system itself is rivaled by the system formed by the multinational corporations.

For his part alone, Means, in the draft of his dissertation (1933, p. 173; see also Lee 1988b, p. 27 note 10), wrote rather colorfully that

> practically self-perpetuating in their dictatorships, invested with tremendous legal powers, becoming increasingly dominant in their economic might as a larger proportion of industry comes yearly under their sway, the few men in control of the largest corporations threaten to become the uncrowned kings and economic masters of the land.[26]

Indeed, already in their 1932 volume Berle and Means had also written that

> the recognition that industry has come to be dominated by these economic autocrats must bring with it a realization of the hollowness of the familiar statement that economic enterprise in America is a matter of individual initiative. To the dozen or so men in control, there is room for such initiative. For the tens and even hundreds of thousands of workers and of owners in a single enterprise, individual initiative no longer exists. Their activity is group activity on a scale so large that the individual, except he be in a position of control, has dropped into relative insignificance. At the same time the problems of control have become problems in economic government. (1932, pp. 124–125)

Apropos thereof, Commons's summary and interpretation of Berle and Means addresses "the hierarchy of 'economic governments' " (1950, p. 325) and "the delegation of legislative power to private corporations" (p. 301); see also p. 328: "Berle and Means have investigated the present status of the delegation of legislative authority to private corporations. . . ." Commons also echoes Vilfredo Pareto and Robert Michels in the matter of an inevitable tendency toward oligarchy: "Historical investigations in these related fields might show an almost inevitable tendency—call it 'economic determinism'—toward centralized management and 'dictatorship,' away from 'democracy,' " (p. 319), a view, of course, also close to that of Schumpeter (1942). Commons and his student, Selig Perlman, advanced the distinction between opportunity consciousness and job consciousness to distinguish between types of actual economic opportunity sets (and the respective perceptions of and attitudes toward them). They believed, therefore, that

> personal freedom could be abridged or invaded by denial of economic facilities offered or provided by privately owned enterprises. Such facilities indeed were chiefly in private hands—overwhelmingly, in fact, offered or conducted by corporations. Yet they were essential to life and personality. (Berle in Berle and Means 1968, p. xviii)

Berle could argue that

> The emerging principle appears to be that the corporation, itself a creation of the state, is as subject to constitutional limitations which limit action as is the state itself. (Ibid., p. xvii)

The problem is in part that when rights conflict, any given state action can be seen quite differently: as protection of private rights (of Alpha) or as intrusion upon private rights (of Beta). The late Arthur Selwyn Miller (see, for example, Samuels and Miller 1987, chapter 10) developed the theme that the corporation should be more explicitly constitutionalized. To some this has meant an intrusion on the rights and power of the corporation; to others, the control of the corporation; to still others, either or both of the foregoing but also the still higher elevation of the corporation to the status of governance, as has been true of private property itself. The point here is that, whatever the course of constitutionalizing the corporation and however one views government in relation to private rights, the corporation is, as Means and Berle early understood, already an important part of the total socioeconomic system of organization and control, that is, of governance.

3

A New Microeconomics

If by microeconomics one means the study of the allocation of resources at the level of the individual economic unit and transaction, then Gardiner Means had a conception of how the microeconomy operates that is fundamentally at variance with that held by most mainstream economists and certainly that manifest by the Chicago School—except, in this latter regard, in one fascinating respect. Means believed that many prices, perhaps most prices, not solely those in the oligopoly core of the economy, were administered. Many prices were formed in ways that differed fundamentally from the way presumed by and portrayed in the mainstream theory of flexible prices (in both its Marshallian and Walrasian variants). Means also had a quite different view of the price adjustment process and of the firm in its relation to the market from the view held by mainstream theorists.

1. Administered Prices

There is no conclusive independent test of when a price is set by administration and when by the market; all prices are enunciated by people; markets do not issue price lists. There also is no conclusive independent test of when a price is flexible and when inflexible.

That, we think, must be taken as a given in the state of the discipline, perhaps a permanent condition. Beyond that, it seems accurate to say that many economists believe that all prices are sufficiently flexible to be called flexible; that many other economists believe that many prices are sufficiently inflexible to be called inflexible, whereas many other prices are effectively flexible; and that many economists, including some of the immediate foregoing, believe that many prices are flexible upward but relatively inflexible downward. There is now, too, a substantial literature, within the mainstream if not center stream, in microeconomics as well as macroeconomics (including the microeconomic foundations of macroeconomics), which explores sticky, fixed or inflexible prices, as well as modes of competition other than those based on price.

In addition, there are those economists, perhaps the great majority, who see prices, however generated and however characterizable in terms of flexibility, as simple yet complex coefficients of choice, or as essentially episodic resting points in the eternal dance between supply and demand. There are other economists who envision prices as weapons in the complex struggle between protagonists for the market, sometimes predatory but sometimes, perhaps more often, not; but always calculated and conveying situational meaning. Economics is thus in these respects a set of stories embodying various beliefs about pricing and prices.

Contrary to the traditional imagery of markets continously moving toward (or, in the Walrasian view, effectively in) market clearing, through competitive prices sensitive enough to register all sorts of marginal alterations in market conditions, Gardiner Means believed that the reality of prices was very different and much more complex. Means considered it to be an erroneous assumption that prices are always determined by the interaction of buyers and sellers and that they change in a highly flexible manner. He rejected as either vague or completely inaccurate the conventional view that prices are determined by the market (perhaps "in" the market but not "by" the market).[27] Anticipatory or evocative of Coase's already quoted, later statement about "blackboard economics," Means criticized the "false clearness" of the "customary crossed lines of supply and demand'' curves in the textbooks, a product of the assumption of perfectly flexible prices (Means 1933, p. 125).

The core of Means's view resides in his conception of a trade or of trading. He considered the oriental bazaar that he observed in Turkey to constitute the typical example of a true trade. It is a process of buying and selling, and ''buying and selling is essentially a matter of trading in the sense of getting the best price. Price does not *precede* a trade, but is determined in a trade and therefore flexibility of price can be assumed to exist. An equating of supply and demand at the market price[28] can be posited without too great a distortion of the facts and the whole economic process can be summed up as an intricate system of trades'' (Means 1933, p. 131).[29] In the overwhelming majority of conventional markets in developed economies, on the contrary, ''*prices are fixed by administrative action for periods of time*'' and ''*supply and demand never equate except by coincidence*'' (p. 135). Moreover, ''Whereas there may be a tendency for the proportionate discrepancy between supply and demand to decrease in the long run, there is *no* tendency for the absolute amount of the discrepancy to decrease. One must, therefore, say that the supply and demand curves which so neatly cross in the economist's traditional description of the market cannot be employed to describe this market'' (p. 140). His example is ''the typical department store market'' where ''it is almost inconceivable that each transaction . . . should be a matter of higgling and bargaining between the shop girl and the customer'' (p. 135). The department store case is also a good example of his general critical position: affirmation of how real-world markets operate, not opposition to markets per se. ''The modern corporation,'' Means wrote in the summary of his dissertation (Means 1962a, p. 18), not only brought ''a greater part of economic activity within the administrative limits of single units, but has altered the character of the market by making *price* not an outgrowth of trading but of administration.''

In partial support of this view, which depends principally on his empirical understanding of what goes on in actual markets compared to a situation of hypothetical pure trading, Means early stressed the indeterminacy of cost due to the phenomenon of joint costs, especially in the context of the great modern corporation in which "production is the result of a functioning, interrelated organization. In the large corporation, direct, easily attributable costs are at a minimum." Moreover,

> the arbitrariness of the allocation of the costs lumped into overhead increases as these assume a larger proportion in relation to total costs. The long-winded arguments over the problem of depreciation suggest that clarity in corporate accounting will not be developed until the whole process represented by corporate enterprise is treated as a continuous process of joint costs with the cost of any product, or even of large categories of products, thoroughly indeterminate. Nor can the economist hope to aid this clarification unless he in turn accepts joint cost as a fundamental postulate. (Means 1933, pp. 149–150)

Means also questioned whether, in understanding price policy or price determination, the combination of competition and profit maximization is both a sufficient regulator and an adequate explanation of profits "where the great modern corporations are concerned" (p. 174).

His principal argument, however, lay elsewhere.[30] According to Means, the important prices are (1) set in an administrative context and (2) generally relatively inflexible. As for the first, prices in the great corporations that dominate the economy are set administratively. Precisely how they are set requires close study, something which economists typically have not pursued, and something of which firms typically prefer to deny scrutiny. One variant is markup pricing, in which a pre-established percentage is added to calculated unit costs. Another is target return pricing or budgeted profits, in which case, perhaps using linear programming or optimal control theory, firms consider their revenue, cost and tax functions, and their schedules of desired dividends, retained earnings, and pay-out ratio, for various levels of output and corresponding alternative prices, aiming to produce the output quantity at the corresponding price that will yield the desired level of after-tax, after-dividends retained earnings. Typically this is calculated with consideration to cash flow, growth rate, and market share factors as well as corporate survival. Complicated and administrative, this is the price-determination black box more or less opened up. In any event, Means considered that economic organization was coordinated by both competition (in various forms) and administration; by neither alone, but by both.

Means was aware that the administration of prices in practice was both extremely diverse and complex. Insisting that there is "a sharp, easily-defined, and easily-observed distinction between prices made in the market and prices which are set and held constant for a period of time and a series of transactions," Means found in the latter category "(a) a great range in the frequency of price changes and (b) a notably high proportion . . . which change infrequently." He acknowledged that "there is no objective basis for defining or observing the distinction between frequent and infrequent so that the division is either varied from purpose to purpose or is given an *arbitrary* dividing line." Moreover, some administered prices are sensitive to changes in demand or costs and thus "can approximate the classical market behavior and may raise no practical issues." He wanted to advance "the *fact* of price administration which conflicts with existing theory" and the "general thesis that it is better to make 'administered price' the term applied to the whole category of prices which change frequently or infrequently and are fairly sensitive or insensitive to changes in demand or costs but differ from market prices in that they are set and held constant for periods of time and a series of transactions" (Means to John Blair, undated, pp. 1, 2, 3).

"In our actual economy," Means wrote, "some prices meet the classical flexibility, some are quite inflexible at least for considerable periods, and some have an intermediate degree of flexibility" (Means to Jerry Cohen, 20 March 1964, p. 4). There were different and varying degrees of market pressure, from rivals and from other products with relatively high cross-elasticities of demand. There were nonprice dimensions of competition, or rivalry. There were various measurable degrees of price flexibility. Especially the last; in seeking to substantiate his claim that there were differences as to flexibility in general between agricultural and industrial prices and between varied groupings of industrial prices, Means devoted a great deal of attention to statistical studies of prices. He was able to study only one particular industry in great depth, that being steel (Means 1962b), but he considered, on the basis of his empirical studies as well as his conjectures, that administered pricing was a critical phenomenon which governed both the coordination and performance of the economy.

The prices that count were, in his view, relatively inflexible. Accordingly, adjustments to market changes were typically made in terms of changes in quantity of output:

> Once the individual enterprise has determined on its prices, it will hold these prices constant and vary the flow of output in the light of the demand at these prices, changing its prices only occasionally as conditions change so greatly as to exceed some threshold. (Means 1962b, p. 200; see Lee 1988a, p. 19)

It should be clear, as Frederic Lee has emphasized, that, for Means, "the demise of the principle of supply and demand in determining prices [for the great corporations] rested primarily upon the mere size of the corporate enterprise, as opposed to the separation of ownership from control" (Lee 1988c, p. 21)—though, of course, size itself is dependent upon that separation, and vice versa.

For Means, certain features of the modern corporate economy which we take for granted are arrangements which are time and space specific. Apropos of the economic valuation of property, whereas hitherto the value of a going concern depended on the negotiations between willing buyer and seller of an individually, personally operated enterprise, now the values of corporate securities depend on the economic machinery of the securities markets (Commons 1950, p. 306). Similarly, whereas pure prices to Means depended on the literal haggling between buyer and seller in the market, in practice they predominantly mean prices set on a take-it-or-leave-it basis by one party, typically the seller, with the prices set within the firm somehow generated in an administrative fashion and more or less resistant to change.

It was Means's view that the modern mass market—typified by the department store—required that prices be set by one party as part of a standardized contract of adhesion.[31] The transaction costs of regular negotiations between buyers and sellers in that department store, for example, would be prohibitive. Indeed, modern buyers and sellers did not seem to miss the turmoil of haggling in markets. The modern economy was a different way of life from one in which prices arose via bargaining within the context of each transaction. The modern economy was one in which prices might be affected by market forces, but it was also one in which prices were largely set administratively.[32]

Means was principally concerned with markets in which standardized commodities were sold. He did not deny the existence of transaction-specific prices in the case of customized commodities—though even in these markets he believed that administration rather than market was predominant, in the rules used to form the prices.

Means was aware, from the very beginning, of the major qualifications that others might bring to bear on his analysis. He acknowledged that administered prices are generally list prices and that contract prices can and do differ therefrom. But he believed that even departures from list prices were administered, that is, were conducted within administered ranges or made on the basis of administrative policy. The relative inflexibility of list prices thus carried over to contract pricing.[33] The same is true of collateral features or terms of contracts; these, too, were undertaken on the basis of administrative policy.

Interestingly, in these matters both Means and his critics portray an economy very different from both the hypothetical Walrasian tâtonnement process and the usual images of autonomous entities engaging in fleeting transactions in mechanistic, impersonal, automatic markets. The mainstream image of voluntary exchange between isolated simple individuals subject to the elaborate hegemony of competition, with no individual actor having any control over price, differs, for Means, fundamentally from the reality of rivalry, structural limits to competition, and adhesion contracts set in advance for a period by one actor or the other. For Means, administered prices are not totally independent of market forces and concerns, but they are not generally subject to real bargaining.[34] Rather they are manipulated within a zone of discretion open to the firm—a zone of discretion totally ignored by "blackboard economics," except perhaps in the case of limit-entry pricing, which to Means seems to have been only a small aspect of the larger practice.

Means was willing to attribute some price inflexibility to labor unions, but insisted that inflexible administered prices both antedated and were more systemic than that.

> Administered prices and their relative inflexibility are not a product of labor organization. Before 1933, labor unions played a very minor role in most American industry and yet both prices and wage rates in such industries as steel and automobiles were administered and relatively inflexible. Both prices and wage rates were administered by management, presumably as a single policy. . . . The subsequent organization of labor may well have increased the inflexibility of administered prices but price administration grows out of the structure of our industrial economy and the character of its markets regardless of the degree of labor organization. (Means to Jerry Cohen, 20 March 1964, p. 3)

It is important to recognize that in at least one respect Means's analysis is quite traditional: he assumed that corporate managers were economically rational. Thus Munkirs (1988, p. 36) argues that "Means' administered price hypothesis contained four fundamental propositions." They are:

> First, the prices of goods and services produced in industries where output was concentrated in a few firms would not be set by competitive impersonal market forces, but, rather, would be administered by businessmen.

> Second, Means contended that there was a direct and close relationship between the number of times a firm changed its prices and the magnitude of its price increases or decrease. . . .
>
> Third, Means argued that in the country's concentrated industries declining consumer demand had been countered by decreasing production and employment while maintaining stable prices. . . .
>
> Finally, Means, as did Chamberlin and Robinson, adopted the people neutrality concept. Administered prices were to be viewed simply as rational economic behavior on the part of individual businessmen, given the existence of corporate micro-market power. (pp. 36–37)

The third and fourth points anticipate the application of Means's work to macroeconomics, considered below. The final point underscores both the conventionality of his general emphasis on rational economic behavior and his nonconventionality in seeking to identify precisely what such behavior meant in the real world of the modern corporation.

Means's work was also conservative in the sense of nonrevolutionary in one critical respect: his acceptance of the corporation, the corporate system, and administered pricing:

> I regard administered prices as *a good thing*. They make for economic efficiency. I doubt if we could have the efficiencies of modern industry without administered prices. The big mass-production corporations could not operate without administered prices. . . . Business could not do its planning as effectively as it does and the super market would be impossible without administered prices. That administered prices make the main body of nineteenth century economic theory obsolete is the hard luck of those who only know how to teach that body of theory. But administered prices are a good thing from the point of view of the people of this country provided we understand and meet the problems which they create and which lie outside the scope of traditional economic theory. (Means to Jerry Cohen, 20 March 1964, p. 2; see also p. 8: "administered prices are essential to efficient modern business.")

2. The Price Adjustment Process

The centerpiece of Means's approach to microeconomics (and by implication to macroeconomics) is the predominance of administered prices which tend to be inflexible in practice. Because of variations in definition, data acquisition, and manipulation, and variations in otherwise operationalizing these ideas (some problems arising from the ideas and materials themselves and some from differences in ideology and/or paradigm), quite diverse conclusions are reached in the relevant literature (see chapter 5). One implication of Means's analysis, perhaps theoretically and practically the most far-reaching implication, has to do with the price adjustment process with regard to *both* price structure and general price level. It is Means's fundamental contention that the price adjustment or coordination mechanism does not operate smoothly, indeed, that it operates quite erratically and dysfunctionally because of the differential lags involved in the adjustment of various prices to changed conditions and to each other, due in part to the administration of prices.

This view conflicts especially with the Walrasian story of how markets ultimately may be said to work—the fiction of the auctioneer and the pretense that trading does not take place until prereconciled equilibrium prices have been established—but it also conflicts with the mechanistic adjustment process of Marshallian price theory. From Means's point of view, it is the combination of seeking determinate equilibrium solutions plus the "blackboard economics" of conventional demand and supply analysis which has prevented most economists from appreciating and analyzing the adjustment process and thus from learning how it is in fact that prices are worked out. He called, not surprisingly, for "a reexamination of the processes and mechanisms of economic adjustment assumed by traditional economic theory . . . " (Ware 1988a, p. 1). In mainstream economics, in his view, "there was little concern as to how administered prices were actually set—what considerations corporate executives actually used in determining prices within the range of discretion which they could exercise and what mechanisms they employed. Such inquiries as were made were often stonewalled by corporations as business secrets to which only the company insiders were privy. Economists did not develop tools of analysis to penetrate this area'' (Ware 1988a, p. 8).

Means did not believe that ''the free enterprise system is a cybernetic mechanism'' which automatically equates demand and supply and thus clears markets, eliminates unemployment, balances international payments, and distributes income in accordance with productivity. Rather, the classical automatic adjustment mechanism ''is obsolete for an economy dominated by administered prices.'' The point is that ''if there were no administered prices or wage rates and all prices and wage rates were made in the market and adjusted quickly to equate supply and demand,'' there would be no adjustment or coordination problems. In the presence of administered prices and wages, moreover, the old gold standard and the specie flow mechanism would ''operate primarily through relative changes in employment, not through changes in the price-wage level except possibly very slowly'' (Means to Jerry Cohen, 20 March 1964, pp. 1, 4, 5; see also p. 7 regarding ''a much slower upward revison of administered prices corresponding to the rise in unit costs . . . ''). ''The failure of the automatic price-level adjustment is easily explained by the inflexibility of administered prices'' (Means in Berle and Means 1968, p. xxxiv).

Most of Means's attention in these matters was devoted to what he called administered inflation, which has become, as will be discussed below, the heart of the Post Keynesian approach to explaining inflation. The core of the argument is that competition is highly imperfect in the world of the modern corporation in which businesses administer prices, and that the prices are generally, however variably, inflexible. As a consequence, the price adjustment process is stretched out and, in contrast with the model of perfect adjustment, is distorted: price need no longer equate demand and supply. In the traditional theory, abnormal profits will induce entry of new competitors who, by offering additional supplies, will lower prices. ''But where prices are administered, it is quite likely that'' the new entrants ''will open up for business *at the existing administered price* and try to take business away from the existing competitors by advertising and other forms of promotion.'' Eventually ''each producer's profits go down, partly because of the rise in unit costs and partly because of the smaller number of units it sells. . . . Excessive profits have been eliminated, not by lower prices but by increasing waste of resources both through excessive promotion and through excessive use of capital and management skills.'' Moreover, ''it is not yet clear under what conditions, if any[,] the competition from easy entry will reduce profits to competitive levels by reducing administered prices. . . . With administered prices and easy entry, competition can be expected to control excessive profits but is quite as likely to do this by increasing costs toward price as by reducing price toward costs'' (Means to Jerry Cohen, 20 March 1964, pp. 7–8).[35]

There is a wide range or variety of prices and not all function to clear markets in an orderly, and certainly not in a synchronous, fashion. As a result, a plethora of microeconomic and macroeconomic problems develop: noncoordination, miscoordination, inefficiency, and instability. Adjustments in administrative prices cannot be supposed necessarily to coordinate or to clear markets by equating demand and supply at either the microeconomic or the macroeconomic level. The adjustment and coordination mechanism-process is neither instantaneous nor fully effective in the presence of administered prices. Along with other Post Keynesian economists Means maintained that mainstream neoclassical economists have not much studied the adjustment process and only assume that it works either instantaneously or otherwise. Administered pricing is but one reason for the failure of prices to adjust and coordinate (uncertainty, lengthy contracts, acceleration and multiplier relationships, transaction costs, and variations in decision-making and production processes are other causes); but it is, for Means, the principal cause. Not all prices adjust at the same rate, in any case, but the presence of administered prices means that the less flexible prices lag behind the more flexible, and maladjustment is both generated and aggravated. There was not for Means any belief in ready equilibrium, frictionless markets, and perfect coordination and adjustment. Administrative prices may coordinate, but in a dramatically different fashion and with considerably different results from those that transpired in the logical picture provided by the conventional hypothetical economy of fully flexible prices. As Lee notes (1988a, p. 28), for Means the existence and interdependence of the market and the administered sectors prevents the coordination of economic activity solely through price adjustments—which points to the importance of quantity changes and thus substantive economic instability.

One final aspect of administered pricing and the price adjustment process: As Hodgson (1988, pp. 125, 130, and passim) has stressed, inflexible prices (and quantities) can be due to the predominance of routinized procedures and practices within businesses. "As George Shackle (1972, p. 227) argues in his chapter on 'prices as conventions,' prices which 'have stood at particular levels for some time acquire thereby some sanction and authority' " (Hodgson 1988, p. 184). As Hodgson (1988, p. 190) also points out, Kregel (1980, p. 46) treats administered prices as an uncertainty-reducing institution.

3. The Theory of the Firm in Relation to the Market

In addition to administered prices and the price adjustment process, another central element of Gardiner Means's microeconomics consists of his belief that ours is a dual economy comprised of market and administrative sectors in which the policies and actions of corporate management are distinctly responsible for the division of activity between the two sectors. This is a remarkable view; it does not posit the market as independent of and transcendental to the firm, but contemplates the market as emerging from the same process as does the firm itself—and as a result, in part, of decisions made within the firm.

Consider the following: What is the rationale for the firm and what determines the range of activities it undertakes? Is there not a "cost of using the price mechanism," a "cost of carrying out a transaction by means of an exchange on the open market?'' It can be argued that ''although production could be carried out in a completely decentralized way by means of contracts between individuals, the fact that it costs something to enter into these transactions means that firms will emerge to organize what would otherwise be market transactions whenever their costs were less than the costs of carrying out the transactions through the market. The limit to the size of the firm is set where its costs of organizing a transaction become equal to the cost of carrying it out through the market.'' The development of the firm in this manner constitutes ''planning within our economic system which is quite different from . . . individual planning and which is akin to what is normally called economic planning. . . . [It is] typical of a large sphere in our modern economic system.'' Coordination by the price system is not necessary. ''Within a firm . . . market transactions are eliminated, and in place of the complicated market structure with exchange transactions is substituted the entrepreneur-co-ordinator, who directs production. It is clear that these are alternative methods of co-ordinating production.'' Moreover, ''the degree to which the price mechanism is superseded varies greatly. . . . the amount of 'vertical' integration, involving as it does the supersession of the price mechanism, varies greatly from industry to industry and from firm to firm.'' But the critical matter is ''that the distinguishing mark of the firm is the supersession of the price mechanism. . . . [C]o-ordination is the work of the price mechanism in one case and of the entrepreneur in another.'' That is the Chicago view of Ronald Coase, initially published in 1937 and republished and reaffirmed in 1988 (Coase 1988, pp. 6–7, 35–37). It makes administration the correlative of the market and managerial decisions the principal, at least proximate, determinant of the division of activity between administration and market.[36] As Hodgson (1988, p. 199)[37] puts it, for Coase ''the key feature of the firm is its internal 'suppression of the price mechanism' . . . and the allocation of resources by command rather than price.''

And that, with one qualification, is precisely the view held by

Gardiner Means.[38] For Means, not only are prices administered within the modern giant corporation; so also are both the domain of the firm itself and the division of activity between corporate administration and the market.

In the draft of his doctoral dissertation Means wrote that the separation of ownership and control eliminated the barrier hitherto posed by the wealth of the individual owner to further extension of the size of the enterprise. "Both . . . the separation of labor from control and of the owner from control . . . have made possible the continuing development in the size of the individual enterprise, have reduced the area within which the economic process is organized through the interplay of prices and have increased the area within which production is organized . . . and the coordination of production on a planned basis" (Means 1933, p. 6). He argued that we have an economy "in which within large areas, production is organized on an administrative . . . basis and *in which the markets on the [periphery] of these areas take on an engineering character as price becomes a matter of administration rather than a matter of trading*" (p. 134, emphasis in original).[39] In the summary of the dissertation, Means wrote:

> Earlier writers have recognized that economic activity is only in part trading and that the element of administration enters in, but they have tended to minimize this administrative aspect. The modern corporation has not only increased this aspect by bringing a greater part of economic activity within the administrative limits of single units, but has altered the character of the market by making *price* not an outgrowth of trading but of administration. (Means 1962a, p. 18)

This also is the view advanced, for example, in Galbraith's *New Industrial State* (1967) and, more recently, by Paul Weaver, who is quoted by a reviewer as arguing that "the corporation believes in managing markets rather than freeing them; in shaping the rules of the game to its advantage, rather than competing under rules made by others; in staking out a protected new market or niche rather than competing toe to toe with other manufacturers"

(Rothenberg 1988, p. 40). As Taussig might put the matter, the corporation will endeavor to brook no interference by market or competitor with its sphere of autonomy and domination and will indeed also endeavor to extend that sphere.

This view of Coase, Means, and others represents one half of a bifurcated neoclassical conception of the firm and its management.[40] Sometimes the firm and its administrators are portrayed as passive responders to market signals; they are the conduit through which consumer sovereignty works via markets. At other times, so neatly represented here, the firm and its management are portrayed as active agents of change—in one sense or another as dynamic entrepreneurs. They are the dynamic force in economic change. It seems that to both Coase and Means, as well as to others, a key aspect of the relation of the firm to the market is that corporate administration (for Coase, presumably that of any firm) determines the division of activity between firm and market and thereby helps determine the domain of the market. No longer is it simply the case that the firm operates in the given market; the firm now helps determine wherein the market will operate in relation to that firm.

The matter has been nicely expressed by Lee (1988b, 1988c), though not in relation to Coase:

> [Means] argued that administration and coordination of economic activities by management had replaced the coordination of economic activities by the forces of supply and demand in the market place. That is, the large corporation had internalized production activities that were once found in the market and subject[ed] them to administrative coordination, while also entering directly into the market to coordinate activities on its own behalf [citations deleted]. (Lee 1988b, p. 16; 1988c, p. 18)

Lee also writes that for Means, ''management could continuously reorganize itself so as to make itself efficient at any scale of production''; that ''management, in its drive to have the corporation grow larger, could internalize many former market activities while taking on new ones by employing a bureaucracy to coordinate them''; and that for Means ''the importance of organizational controls in a corporate economy was due precisely to the rise of economic groups and institutions who could manage their affairs largely independent of the market.'' In a still larger context he quoted Means thus:

> The great shift from a dominantly agricultural to a dominantly industrial economy during the last century has tended to expand organizational controls. The increased concentration of production into large corporate units, expansion of government functions, increased financial concentration, and growth of both labor organizations and trade associations all work in this direction. The expansion in the role of organization has reduced the relative importance of market controls and increased that of nonmarket controls to such an extent that market controls no longer dominate economic activity. (Lee 1988a, p. 18; p. 55 note 37, quoting Means 1939, p. 155)[41]

It seems to us that this theory of the relation of the firm to the market, for all of its surprising parallel Chicago construction, both elaborates Means's general idea of the corporate system and constitutes a major element of his microeconomic analysis of that system. That Chicago economists, such as George Stigler, have had little or nothing good to say about Means's work, especially administered pricing, despite the logical implication that price administration is part of the separation of the firm from the market (or replacement of the market by the firm) *à la* Coase, is, then, a great irony. There seem to be two Chicagos when it comes to the theory of the firm in relation to the market.

Another way of looking at the matter, one also consistent with Coasian analysis, is to say that managerial discretion is limited by transaction costs. If ''transaction costs bear directly on the extent to which managers can exercise discretion in their own interest rather than their stockholders', because information, bargaining, and monitoring costs can prevent stockholders from banding together effectively to control the managers'' (Sherman 1974, pp.

155–156), then the same is true of managerial ability to replace the market. But the existence of transaction costs negates neither managerial discretion nor the replacement phenomenon, it only channels them.

We have already noted the minor qualification that for Coase the separation-replacement argument applies in principle to all firms. We qualify even that by saying that the same is arguably true for Means as well. For both men, it is true for every firm insofar as the firm can accomplish separation-replacement in the Coase-Means sense. For Means, at any rate, this is explicitly within the power of the management of the modern corporation, especially the giants among them, and these are not excluded (though not so concentrated upon) by Coase.

It is undoubtedly also true that no Chicago school economist would agree with Means that "competition as the faithful watchdog standing guard over the national income to prevent its diversion into the hands of the powerful becomes, perhaps, an economic myth" (Means 1933, p. 175; also quoted in Lee 1988b, p. 28 note 11). There is considerable irony and also ambiguity in this as well. Chicago economists fundamentally believe that markets are by their very nature competitive. But where does the Coase (or Means-Coase) theory of the firm in relation to the market leave that belief? Perhaps Chicago and Means are in effective agreement that the modern giant corporation has twin features: it operates within a range of insulated discretion, even in its opportunities to replace the market; and that range is itself constrained by the market, that is, by competitive or competition-like forces in the market. Means never asserted that administration totally replaces the market even in the administered sector, and neither certainly has Coase.

The major difference between Means's and Coase's views of the relation of the firm to the market resides elsewhere, and it, too, is not absolute. It appears to be this: Means was not willing to rationalize every business decision as presumptively optimal for both the firm and the economy. Means believed—and he is much more conservative in this than most people seem to have appreciated—that the corporate system had to be accepted as such, but only so long as it was recognized to exist and so long as it came to operate within a legal system capable of transmuting its self-interested operation into some legally-politically determined public interest. Coase, on the other hand, seemed much more willing to accept as per se optimal for both the firm and the economy any business decisions, even those that replace the market with the firm—though his acceptance was apparently not absolute. Once again we encounter for Chicago, and also for Means, the possible hiatus between business decision and the market, so far as both the presumptive welfare status of the former and implications for the competitiveness of the latter are concerned. Means, at any rate, makes it quite clear that the legal-political process will have to work out answers to the questions generated by the hiatus. It seems to us that Chicago does likewise but does not make much of it, though the economists of that school do go out of their way to minimize state action of all types. For Means, however, necessary, pragmatic, and democratic state action was the preferred alternative to both economic chaos and fascistic or communistic order. This is all in addition to, but in a fundamental sense a qualification of, his belief that "administered prices are essential to efficient modern business" (Means to Jerry Cohen, 20 March 1964, p. 8).

One further matter: The perennial response of the Chicago school to Gardiner Means has been to deny the existence and/or importance of concentration, administered pricing, the separation of ownership and control, and so on. The striking thing is that Chicago now seems implicitly to accept the idea of the separation of ownership and control, but interprets it within its version of the neoclassical paradigm using theories of agency, transaction costs, and a market for control. Absent the separation of ownership and control, a market for control would be irrelevant; introducing the idea of a market for control has the effect of sanitizing what would otherwise be a dangerous idea.

Thus, for both Means and Coase it would appear that neither firms nor markets are natural in the sense of constituting independently existing and self-subsisting entities. Firms, markets, and prices are human artifacts and the modes of their substantive determination have to be explained. For both men, the market is not the sole regulator of economic activity; for Means, especially, it is not the sole determining process generating prices.

The size of the firm is limited by the ability of management to administer its market-replacing activities successfully. Both prices and the division of activity between administration and market are the result in part of conscious decisions, not matters of the independent, impersonal market alone. Means's, and presumably Coase's, analysis is not simply that market forces are limited in concentrated industries. It is "that the decision making process by corporate executives is a major form of intervention into the traditional processes of the free market" (Ware 1988a, p. 18). It is that the market is replaced through self-conscious decisions of firm management. Economic performance is governed not by the market alone but by both the market and corporate administration and by the specific decision making and other rules operative in each, but of course especially the latter—in which at least to some extent the role of profit was either undermined or given selective substantiation. If the dual economy involves a multifaceted and kaleidoscopic interplay between corporate sector-administrative and market-competitive spheres, the interplay is dramatically present at the level of the individual firm.

Both this interplay and the administration of prices, which for Means was so important, were critical parts of what amounts to a new microeconomics. In this new microeconomics there would, for Means, still be a place for managerial profit-maximizing responses to changing corporate situations. Profit maximizing as such appears to be and is worked out within management, not in "blackboard economics."

Whether the effects of decisions for the replacement of market by firm are considered optimal or not, is another question. Any view which either presumptively accepted or rejected such effects would be most conspicuously a function of additional normative premises, but the microeconomic analysis would be very different indeed from that prevalent today—as indeed would the macroeconomic analysis, to which we now turn.

4

The Macroeconomic Consequences of Administered Prices

1. Introduction

In the field of macroeconomics Gardiner Means is best known for his extension of the administered pricing argument to the explanation of exacerbated contraction during the Great Depression and of both inflation and stagflation during the post–World War II period. In order to interpret Means's place in the history of macroeconomic thought, several preliminary considerations need to be raised.

1. Say's Law can be said to rest on four key assumptions: that money serves only as a means of exchange; that the interest rate equates saving and investment; that all prices are flexible; and that wants are insatiable.

2. Keynes's argument in the *General Theory* can be variously interpreted relative to the assumptions of Say's Law, the assumption being rebutted depending on the interpretation given. Emphasis can be given to money as a store of value and thereby to the role of uncertainty, liquidity preference, and the deferral of expenditure. This emphasis renders any ultimate insatiability irrelevant for practical, short-term purposes, inasmuch as households and firms are under no absolute compulsion to consume and invest, respectively, regardless of market conditions and expectations.[42] Emphasis can be given to changes in income, and not the rate of interest,

bringing about equilibrium between saving and investment. Emphasis can be on prices being not totally, if at all, flexible. From one perspective, Keynes's focus is on the variability of the forces and factors that govern spending, which in turn governs money income, real output, employment, and price levels, in part through focusing on the ex ante disequilibrium between saving and investment as well as on the multiplier. From another, it is on the failure of the presumed adjustment mechanisms, such as the interest rate and/or price flexibility, generating instability in real and/or nominal terms.

3. Post Keynesian analysis is no less diverse than the interpretations of Keynes, but most if not all of that analysis seems to manifest the following themes: (a) While equilibrium analysis can be a useful tool, the actual economy is in fact always in disequilibrium and economists should study actual disequilibrium, the adjustment process, and the forces actually at work in the economy. (b) Prices are not determined universally by demand and supply. While such is the case in some peripheral competitive markets, in the oligopolistic core of the economy prices are determined by the use of a markup percentage over cost (or some other technique, such as target return pricing or linear programming or optimal control) to generate desired levels of dividends plus retained earnings. One result is that short-run prices can be virtually unaffected by shifts in demand. (c) In addition to the foregoing emphasis on industrial structure, other structural factors are also important to macroeconomic performance, such as the distributions of income and wealth, and labor market segmentation. (d) The main determinant of the level of unemployment is the volume of output.[43]

4. Kitchin or NBER reference cycle recessions since World War II have generally manifested varying degrees of stagflation—rising unemployment (along with falling output) and inflation (even if at a lower rate than during expansion)—rather than simultaneous deflation and contraction.

5. Stagflation was not a recognized phenomenon in economics

during the late 1970s.[44] Even in the face of empirical evidence of the twin trends, economists denied the possibility of stagflation. It was argued that no theory even suggested its possibility; and certainly no theory was available to explain it. This turned out to be a great embarrassment for the discipline. Eventually the fact of the simultaneous trends was acknowledged and theories were put forth to explain stagflation, including lines of reasoning which had been around earlier but whose stagflationist implications had not been recognized. One historic line of reasoning, for example, was that if wage rates increased faster than productivity, the price level would rise and both output and employment would fall. Another was that if there was an increase in real production costs (such as what came to be called "a supply shock"), an impaired aggregate supply curve would shift leftward and thus a higher price level would be associated with lower real income and corresponding higher unemployment. A third line of reasoning portrayed a growth of inflationary expectations leading to a shift in the Phillips curve outward to the right, with higher price levels associated with higher rates of unemployment. Another composite explanation included factors leading to inflation combined with other factors leading to unemployment, for example, too rapid an increase in the supply of money coupled with the substitution of capital for labor.

These theories could be combined. The gist of all of them, both individually and collectively, was that the market mechanism did not assure simultaneous price stability and full employment. There was also another, more dramatic, nonneoclassical explanation of stagflation: the dominance of an oligopolistic core practicing administered pricing, in which prices were flexible upwards, perhaps with a lag, but more or less insensitive to contractionary conditions. The administered pricing produced output diminutions and only lower inflation rates, not literal deflation. This Post Keynesian explanation combined the oligopoly core pricing with other perversities in such a manner as to exacerbate the business cycle.

Gardiner Means figures into this complex (and variously interpretable) picture in several significant ways. First, he very early explicitly raised the question of a hiatus between saving and investment. Second, he concentrated on the inflexibility of prices as a cause and/or aggravator of instability, in both real and nominal terms. Third, he stressed structural dualism in the economy, encompassing administered pricing and price inflexibility, and thus perverse price behavior over the cycle, in the oligopoly core, leading to the relative incompetence of conventional monetary and fiscal policies to cope with instability. Fourth, he exhorted his fellow economists to study how large corporations in fact behave over the cycle, in part to understand their internal pricing policies and in part to comprehend the adjustment process actually at work in the economy. Fifth, Means's analysis of administered pricing as an explanation of inflation (what he called the perverse pricing explanation of administrative inflation) constitutes an original formulation of a nonneoclassical microeconomic foundation of macroeconomics.[45]

In none of these respects did Means offer his own explanation as the sole and exclusive one—though he obviously considered his ideas an important part of a complex total explanation, perhaps the most important so far as the post–World War II period is concerned. In these respects, however, Means appears to have been either the first or the quintessential Post Keynesian economist. This does not mean that he was as theoretically sophisticated as Sidney Weintraub, Paul Davidson, or Alfred Eichner, for example—though Means was actually no slouch as a theorist. It does signify that Means's reliance on certain fundamental intuitions dating back to *The Modern Corporation and Private Property* and his *Industrial Prices and Their Relative Inflexibility* (1935), and elaborated through an empiricism guided by those intuitions, enabled him to reach the fundamentals of Post Keynesian economics.

2. Administered Pricing and Inflation

Means believed that administered prices were generally inflexible; not fixed, but much more slow to adjust to market conditions than nonadministered or competitive sector prices. Inflation could be and was in fact, after World War II, due to more than increases in the quantity of money. Inflation could be due to the power that firms with control over prices had to raise their prices as part of their internally generated strategy governing the substance of profit maximization, within the range of their discretion. Inflation could take place during expansion, for reasons not associated with bottlenecks, and approaching full employment, as firms responded to increasing money demand by raising prices relatively more than by increasing output. Inflation could take place during recession as firms contracted output rather than lowering prices, for example, to enhance cash flow. Stagflation could result: simultaneous inflation and contraction with increased unemployment. It all depended not on the market or not on the market alone, but on the response to changed conditions of business management with a zone of discretion, in light of their internal plans and strategies. How firms operated, how management behaved, how management pursued what was for them the substance of profit maximization at the microeconomic level, thus helped govern macroeconomic performance.

Means's central concern in these matters for fifty years centered on the perverse role of administered pricing that results from the position of the modern corporation in the economy. His language, the nuances of his analysis, and the circumstances in and to which he addressed his analysis altered somewhat over the years, and his portrayal is complicated because firm pricing behavior and response is so diverse and variable; but the core of the argument remained substantially unchanged. He was arguably the first to stress the stagflationist character of modern recessions, and he came, after World War II, to focus on administered pricing as a (perhaps the most important but not sole) cause of inflation, utilizing the same reasoning with which he had explained the depth of the Great Depression.

Means was aware as early as the period of his work with Berle of the macroeconomic implications of his and Berle's analyses. In the draft of his dissertation he writes of administered prices being variably resistant to changes in consumer demand, emphasizing, for example, that in certain situations, "the immediate effect is to throw out of use the factors of production rather than to reduce their price" (Means 1933, p. 140). In the dissertation summary he emphasized that "prices fixed over periods of time have replaced flexible prices, and supply as defined by classical economists is seldom equated to demand. Rather, *production* tends to be equated to demand at the fixed prices and a disequilibrium between *supply* and demand results not in a fall in price, but in the failure fully to employ the factors of production, or in their over-employment" (Means 1962a, p. 18). One premise of several writings (for example, Means 1938, 1939) was that resources will flow differently at different levels of employment.

The message could be stated in different ways.[46] A major cause of stagflation is the exercise of discretion-power by oligopolies and unions to raise prices and wages even in the circumstance of recession (Blair et al. 1975). Modern inflation is "of a wholly new kind . . . in which prices increase perversely in response to a fall in demand, thus producing simultaneous inflation and recession, an impossibility under traditional theories" (Means in Blaug 1986, p. 588), a message reiterated in the manuscript and associated notes on which he was working at his death (Means 1988). Inflation is essentially cost-push inflation, such that, for example, inflation could develop very early in an expansion, as well as accelerate as the economy approached full employment. Monetary and fiscal policies could be blunted if not negated by firms raising prices in response to an increase in the money supply and/or expansionary fiscal policy, thus frustrating the desired effect on real output. Efforts to control inflation by monetary measures would worsen unemployment. He always argued that the adjustment process strongly tended to involve more output changes and therefore less employment than had prices been more flexible downward. The price mechanism did not guarantee full employment at any price level: "with administered prices, the classical mechanism of automatic employment adjustment could not operate and therefore is obsolete for an economy dominated by administered prices'' (Means to Jerry Cohen, 20 March 1964, p. 4). The key was downward price inflexibility, or perverse pricing, and this was due to administered pricing.

Frederic Lee, who has extensively analyzed Means's work on administered pricing, believes that Means held the view that corporate management tends to adopt a policy that lets ''the level of market activity regulate the rate of production at the given administered price'' (Lee 1988a, p. 19). For Means, ''once the [corporate] enterprise has determined on its prices, it will hold these prices constant and vary the flow of output in the light of the demand at these prices, changing its prices only occasionally as conditions change so greatly as to exceed some threshold'' (Means 1962b, p. 200; quoted in Lee 1988a, p. 19). In the competitive market sector, according to Means, ''market prices behaved pro-cyclically over the business cycle, while production remained relatively unchanged'' (Lee 1988a, p. 24). Whereas in the administered sector, ''Means argued that administered prices were relatively insensitive to changes in aggregate demand over the course of the business cycle while production was sensitive and reacted in a pro-cyclical manner'' (p. 26). Therefore, writes Lee,

> if the market sector dominated the economy . . . variations in aggregate demand over the business cycle would work themselves out primarily through price adjustments and secondarily through output adjustments, hence through variations in the level of employment. On the other hand, if the administered sector dominated the economy, the coordination of economic activity would not be worked out through price adjustments so as to ensure full employment. (p. 27)

Lee substantiates Means's belief that ''this relative asymmetrical response in prices and production . . . [had been] the central point of his administered price explanation of the Great Depression'' (p. 50 note 27), while eventually coming to emphasize ''administrative inflation'' due to ''the ability of the corporate managers to administer their prices to the market and not to any expansionary forces in the market'' (p. 30; see also Lee 1988c, pp. 23–24, and Lee 1987, pp. 17, 23, 37).

In partial summary, Means emphasized that macroeconomic performance was to no small degree governed by inflexible administered prices and their perverse performance over the business cycle.

3. Means in Relation to Keynes

Chapter 8 of the draft of Means's doctoral dissertation, ''The Modern Corporation and the Process of Saving,'' emphasized what he called the ''duality'' of the process of saving. He begins by citing the ''already . . . well recognized'' fact of ''the increasing extent to which saving in the community is done out of corporate income rather than out of the income of individuals.'' Invoking the separation of ownership and control, Means says of this situation that it ''differs from saving as the economist has been familiar with it in that the individual having an interest in corporate income is not in a position to determine whether or not he will save out of that income. Such decision is made by corporate control.'' (This, of course, is the point later made by Hayek, already cited.) Means goes on to note that corporate saving notwithstanding, ''the postulate of received theory,—that the decision to save and the decision to acquire new capital equipment lie in the same hands,—still holds good. In so far as saving out of corporate income is concerned, corporate control has simply supplanted the private entrepreneur'' (Means 1933, p. 152; see also Means 1962a, pp. 18–19).

But, Means argues,

> with respect to the savings of individuals, this postulate no longer holds. The separation of ownership and control has separated the customary process of saving into two independent stages under the control of separate groups of individuals. On the one hand, the decision to save lies in the hands of individuals in the community who ''save''

> through buying corporate securities. On the other hand, the decision to add to the capital goods of corporations, and, correspondingly, to issue new securities with which to supply the funds for this expansion, lies in the hands of control. This means that we have two independent processes going on which by no means necessarily mesh. . . . (1933, pp. 152–153)

Means then goes on to critique Keynes's *Treatise on Money*, citing D. H. Robertson, that Keynes confused "real capital" and "loan capital," arguing that "these values not only may be quite different, but may move in opposite directions" (1933, p. 153). Means also goes on to indicate that savings may be used simply to drive up the prices of already existing securities (p. 155). Lee (1988b, p. 12) traces the basic idea of a hiatus between saving and investment to the idea of the emergence of passive and active property. So far as economic instability is concerned, the recognized absence of this hiatus in the case of corporate saving does not lead to greater stability, which is foreclosed for Means by the untoward behavior of administered prices, if for no other reason.

Several themes were advanced, then, by Means which eventually, ironically largely due to Keynes (who, by this time had already to some extent understood the hiatus between saving and investment), came to characterize the Keynesian view of saving: that an act of saving is substantively different from an act of (real) investment, that they are to some extent done by different parties for different reasons, and that saving need not be devoted to (real) investment. (Perhaps implicit is the idea that investment can be financed by means other than current saving, but this is not explicit.)

Means neither here nor elsewhere presents a complete macroeconomic theory, his own "general theory." He did not envision his theory of administered pricing and the idea of a saving-investment hiatus as constituting a complete theory. From the perspective of today, among other things, considerations of uncertainty and of liquidity preference are important—and these may be deemed implicit in Means's early analysis of the use of retained earnings for purposes other than real investment, notably liquidity per se and other forms of portfolio investment. Certainly all this and more is present in subsequent work and is implicit here. In the summary of the dissertation, Means treated chapter 8 as follows:

> It is then suggested that the process of saving has come to be a dual process conducted by two independent groups of individuals, whose actions do not necessarily mesh, with the result that two separate and independent markets exist, one for capital goods and one for interests in capital goods. It is indicated that prices in these markets may move in opposite directions or in the same direction. (Means 1962a, pp. 18–19)

One can forgive the statement about independent markets, and, now that we are enlightened as to the tortuous, halting, and indirect process by which Keynes's system was worked out, we can understand why Means did not fully appreciate all the implications which could follow from the argument in chapter 8. More important, Means did not follow this saving-investment argument in subsequent work.[47]

So far as Means was concerned, then, the failure of the price flexibility assumption of Say's Law was more important than the failure of either the assumption that money was only a medium of exchange or the assumption that the interest rate equated saving and investment. There was, of course, considerable divergence among the interpretations given to Keynes, say, apropos of the assumptions of Say's Law. As already noted, some interpretations stressed uncertainty and the store of value function of money as deferred choice; others, the saving-investment hiatus; and others, relative price inflexibility and thereby the failure of the price mechanism. There is also considerable divergence among answers to the question of what Keynes himself believed.

Means himself believed that Keynes's macroeconomics did not turn on price inflexibility. In his view, as interpreted by his wife, Caroline Ware (1988a, p. 7), "Keynes used examples of inflexible wage rates and prices in his presentation although these were not relevant or necessary to his theory.'' She also reports that, in a 1939 visit by Means and herself to Keynes at his home, ''for the express purpose of clearing up this point,'' they ''received from Keynes a categorical affirmation that his theory was not based on any assumption other than the classical assumption of perfectly flexible prices and wage rates'' (Ware 1988a, footnotes p. 2, note 21).

Means himself includes a report of this meeting (to the same effect) in a 1976 article entitled ''Which Was the True Keynesian Theory of Employment?'' He begins with acknowledgment of Modigliani's having identified ''two quite different theoretical explanations of persistent unemployment in Keynes' *General Theory of Employment, Interest and Money.*''

> The first theory revolved around Keynes' concept of liquidity preference and the effect of interest rates on the willingness or desire of the public to hold money balances. The second theory revolved around money-wage rates and their failure to behave in the classical fashion of equating supply and demand. Either theory *within its own postulates* could explain the failure of Say's Law to operate. One did this at the macro-level of the demand for money balances and the other at the micro-level of specific markets for labor.

Means notes that the first theory became widely accepted in the United States, only to be subsequently called ''bastard Keynesianism'' by Joan Robinson, who preferred the second as the true Keynesian theory (Means 1976, p. 61). Means argues the reverse view. He concludes, after discussing some passages in the *General Theory*, that ''the evidence seems too strong that his theory of employment was a theory based on the relation between interest rates and money, as the title to his book clearly implies'' (Means 1976, p. 62; the account of the meeting with Keynes is on pp. 61–62), and that ''to explain the obvious failure of Say's Law one should recognize that its validity rests on the classical postulate of price and wage flexibility. Once this is accepted, one can turn to the nonclassical behavior of administered prices or of money-wage rates or both. But this would not be a Keynesian explanation. Its logic would not depend *in any way* on Keynes' valuable concept of liquidity preference'' (p. 63).

Such was Means's view. By way of partial contrast (not to be taken as an intent to give the definitive answer to the question in contention), consider first Bronfenbrenner's recent statement that in 1938–39 one of the beliefs he held was that ''the Keynesian and the price-flexibility insights in macroeconomics and monetary policy appeared to me not fundamentally opposed. I felt that they could and should be unified (with substantial aid from imperfect competition) in a way which would eliminate their inconsistencies'' (Bronfenbrenner 1988, p. v; see also pp. 8–9).

Second, consider Torr's (1988, p. 85) statement that ''as an interpretation of the *General Theory*, the general equilibrium fix-price approach is extraordinary. For we have now reached the stage in which investment, the kingpin of the principle of effective demand, has faded into the background.''

Third, consider Samuelson's (1983, p. 217) statement that ''Keynes-cum-Chamberlin-and-Means would have been better than Keynes alone.'' In this connection, notice should be taken of Feiwel's (1988, p. 1740) statement that ''the imperfect competition revolution had no bearing on the Keynesian revolution, though both of them took place at about the same time and in the same place and both involved at least some of the same dramatis personae. This is more than a doctrinal history puzzlement. Had it been otherwise, it would have fundamentally affected the course of the age after Keynes.'' Feiwel's discussion of Michal Kalecki is of interest here in reference to Means. Feiwel writes that ''in contrast to Keynes, Kalecki was not exposed to the academic teaching of competitive theory. He sometimes used perfect competition in exposition, but when he did so he usually warned that it is a most unrealistic assumption'' (p. 1740), and that ''only in the French version of his 1933 essay (in 1935) did Kalecki first note that in a semi-monopolistic economy, the overall price level depends on the monopolies' policy'' (p. 1741). Apropos of the subsequent development of macroeconomics, Milgate (1988, p. 1747), in a discussion of the decline of the IS-LM analysis, writes that "the focus of modern Keynesian economics has shifted over the last couple of decades," the new focus comprising "price rigidity on the one hand versus differential information on the other." Providing one interpretation of the pre-Keynesian situation, Grampp (1986, p. 6) has written that "for some time before Keynes, economists had explained the business cycle as being affected by price rigidity and had done so in a more informative way than Keynes did. They explained the depression phase and unemployment by wage-stickiness and also made it the cause of the upswing by stating money wages rose less than product prices, causing real wages to fall, profits to rise, and output to increase." Apropos of the question of wage-stickiness, McKibbin (1989, p. 5), building on Clarke (1988), points out "how wage-stickiness, which had originally been seen as a kind of social maladjustment, became in *The General Theory* a 'problem' which it was neither practically nor in principle desirable to 'solve.' "

Consider Tobin's (1988, p. 36) recollection of Chamberlin's and Robinson's argument "in the early 1930s that pure competition among agents with no control over their prices should not be, could not be, the central paradigm of microeconomic theory." In his view,

> that revolution withered from neglect, not from refutation. Chamberlin did not push it, because he was temperamentally orthodox; Mrs. Robinson did not push it, because she had bigger and more heretical fish to fry. Neoclassical theorists ignored it, because it was annoyingly intractable in general equilibrium models. Keynes and his followers, both in America and Britain, ignored it and attempted to ground their new macroeconomics on the standard microeconomic foundations of pure competition, hoping to win their ball game on their opponents' home field. That strategy backfired 30 or 40 years later. Although Keynesians of my generation sincerely say that they had always had imperfect or monopolistic competition in mind as their micro-foundations, only recently have serious theoretical attempts begun to formalize this vision. (pp. 36–37)

This statement says a great deal about the role of sociological factors on the development of economics, including economic theory. It also suggests that had Keynesian economists taken Means, among others, seriously, and meaningfully absorbed his ideas in their analyses, modern economic theory may have developed rather differently. Alas.

Further apropos of this, Lee (1988e) has argued that not only did Means propose an alternative body of theory from that of Keynes, with correspondingly different policies, and oppose the Hansenian stagnationalist explanation of the Great Depression, but he also "developed a mathematical/statistical model of the American economy" that was, in Lee's view, "far more robust than the Keynesian models at the time" (p. 2), and at least "not any worse than those put forth by the American Keynesians and in many respects . . . in fact better" (p. 27). According to Lee, the difference between Means and the Keynesians was that the latter fully accepted neoclassical price theory on the micro side while accepting Keynes on the macro side, thus permitting "the Keynesians to continue to believe in two different and partially conflicting bodies of theory and yet still appear to be rational and sane" (p. 28), whereas Means forged his own theoretic micro foundations for his macroeconomics. The Keynesians thus effectively "assumed there was no problem with the coordination of economic activity" (p. 30) on the micro level, notwithstanding the understanding that macro and micro were two sides of the same coin and that macro-level results were generated by micro-level activity. In Lee's view, the crux was "the desire to reject any attack on neoclassical price theory" (p. 29).

Finally, Hodgson (1988, p. 219) writes that "Keynes' theory of long-term investment is not ahistorical. Noting the 'separation between ownership and management which prevails to-day' and the 'development of organised investment markets,' Keynes . . . argues that decisions to invest in financial terms are no longer irrevocable, and are being constantly revalued on the stock market." Keynes, as Hodgson says, thought that this added "to the instability of the system,'' but one can also interpret it as providing a market check on management (in addition to the market for control)—though this was of course not Means's emphasis. Furthermore, Hodgson (1988, p. 222) also notes that the term ''entrepreneur'' is ''not used with sufficient precision in the *General Theory*. In one passage 'the entrepreneur' is the owner-manager of the firm. In another he is an investor on the stock market. In another still the separation of ownership and control is observed, and the process of expectations-formation is split between the financier and the directors of the firm.'' Regarding the formation of the substance of the firm's objective function, Hodgson (1988, p. 224) also notes that ''Keynes only partly came to terms with the fact that the Marshallian entrepreneur is a rare if not extinct species of capitalist. Thus the agency forming expectations within the firm is rarely a single, commanding individual.'' Moreover, in the ''postwar literature on the theory of the firm . . . the descriptive idea of the firm as an entrepreneur is still prominent. This is because economists have continued to believe that the firm has a set of consistent objectives which are the matter of rational calculation, or assumed that the firm performed 'as if ' this were the case.'' The fundamental problem of objective-function formation revealed by Means's work was thus neither effectively emphasized by Keynes nor fundamentally recognized as a problem by postwar neoclassical theorists.

4. Accounting for the Cost of Idle or Excess Capacity

In one of the chapters in his draft dissertation Means argued that because of the jointness of supply, the cost of any product is essentially indeterminate and the allocation of costs between products is essentially arbitrary. At one point Means discussed the cost of goods damaged in the process of production, saying that ''the accountant and business man would not hesitate to impute the total cost simply to the part of the production which consisted of marketable product'' (Means 1933, p. 148). He also says that the problem of joint cost "becomes greatly magnified" in the case of the giant corporation. The key relevant point is that "the arbitrariness of the allocation of the costs lumped into overhead increases as these assume a larger proportion in relation to total costs" (p. 149). Early on, then, Means was aware of the critical question of how alternative valorizations of costs can affect the accounting records on the basis of which business decisions are made.

Needless to say, Means was concerned throughout his career with economic policy. His principal policy views focused on the potential dysfunctionality of traditional monetary and fiscal policies in the face of a dual economy and administered prices, the irrelevance if not undesirability of antitrust actions in the face of the corporate system, the possibility of a budget in principle balanced over the business cycle performing a countercyclical role, and so on. He was always seeking sensitive policy strategies with which to respond to problems of instability under the corporate system and administered pricing, and in this he was flexible and open-minded.

Near the end of his life Means returned to the question of how costs are valorized in accounting and thereby used in business decision making. At his death he had written some three dozen pages articulating a proposal which, if adopted, he seemed to think would eliminate "the new non-monetary source of inflation." By this he meant, of course, the relative inflexibility of prices such that many prices, perhaps an increasing proportion, remain high or even increase in the face of decreased effective demand while production falls.

Means came to understand the problem of perverse pricing as "*the action of a firm with significant pricing discretion that chooses to raise its price when demand falls because of the current cost of maintaining idle capacity which does not contribute to current production*" (Means 1988, chapter 4, p. 10). The problem, then, arises neither because of administered pricing per se nor because of the general inflexibility of prices nor because of the cyclical perversity of prices per se, but because of "*the flaw in the way firms handle the Fixed Costs of Idle Capacity in the process of estimating unit costs when some part of capacity is idle*'' (p. 12).

It is, alas, not entirely clear what Means had in mind by way of a solution. Some passages (for example, chapter 7, p. 38) suggest the use of long-run pricing. Other passages seem to augur a change in accounting practices, for example, where he writes critically of confusing ''the Fixed Costs of Capacity Operated and the Fixed Costs of Idle Capacity'' (chapter 1, p. 4). That the two are facets of the same solution is suggested by his criticism of administrative pricing that shifts ''so much of pricing from the use of Long-Run to Short-Run Pricing Formulas *without adjusting for the peculiar difference between the Fixed Unit Costs of Idle Capacity and the Fixed Unit Costs of Capacity in Use*'' (chapter 1, p. 4). Means proposed to show that ''when either the classical Monopoly Calculus or the Neoclassical Full-Cost Pricing Calculus is applied to Short-Run Pricing it operates to seriously over-state the most profitable price'' (chapter 1, p. 4). There is therefore ''*an Inflationary Bias when a firm's costs include The Costs of Idle Capacity and these costs are not properly treated as a separate cost factor*'' (chapter 2, p. 6). Instead of combining the fixed costs of idle capacity and of capacity in use into a ''single fixed-cost factor,'' Means proposed to treat the former as an ''independent cost factor'' and ''*show how the peculiar relation between the Fixed Costs of Capacity In Use and The Fixed Costs Of Idle Capacity generates an Inflationary Bias under Short-Run Pricing*'' (chapter 2, p. 6A). He objected to what he considered the exaggeration of costs in pricing by introducing the fixed costs of idle capacity ''into the pricing calculus,'' but in a way that ''hides this fact by combining the Fixed Costs of Idle Capacity with the Fixed Costs of Capacity in Use *as if they were interchangeable costs* even though changes in unit costs of idle capacity tend to have quite a different effect from that of changes in the Fixed Cost of Capacity In Use'' (chapter 2, p. 8).

Means seems to have concluded that the inclusion of the fixed costs of idle capacity in pricing gave the economy an inflationary bias, the more so as capacity utilization fell. He seems to be proposing a disaggregation of costs from the conventional two-cost pricing formula of variable and fixed costs to a three-cost pricing formula of variable costs, fixed costs of capacity in use, and fixed costs of idle capacity. He argues that these two formulas, in addition to a one-cost pricing formula with simply reckoned total costs, "would produce *the same Unit Cost* for the firm's product if the firm operated *At Capacity* and so *had no Costs of Idle Capacity*." But the introduction of idle capacity, without giving its costs separate treatment, also causes "the new non-monetary source of inflation, by generating a new source which will be called *Perverse Pricing*" (chapter 2, pp. 12, 13).

We have been unable to identify precisely how Means proposed to solve the problem of inflation exacerbated by including the costs of idle capacity in administered pricing. Obviously he would have had them separately identified. Presumably he would have had firms generate prices either on the basis of the estimated costs of capacity in use or using long run estimates of costs without idle capacity (or without idle capacity greater than planned reserve capacity), but of this we cannot be certain.

Means obviously pointed to an interesting phenomenon: the increase in unit costs of output due to an increase in idle capacity notwithstanding the fact that the cost of idle capacity is not itself strictly speaking part of the cost of actual output—though from the perspective of the long-run survival of the firm all costs must be covered, including the cost of idle capacity. At any rate, Means was still aware of the critical question of how alternative valorizations of costs can affect the accounting records on the basis of which business decisions are made.

5

The Reception of Means's Work and the Relation of His Work to That of Others

1. Introduction

The principal objective of this volume is the interpretation and assessment of Gardiner Means's work. Part of this task necessarily involves consideration of the reception given to Means's work and of the relation of his work to that of others. There are two overriding aspects of the situation: first, the great diversity of reception and the wide variances of evaluation given his work in the literature; second, the vastness of the literature on the multiplicity of very substantial topics on which Means wrote.

Most of this chapter and the next deals with the former aspect. Nevertheless, any attempt to interpret and assess Means's work must touch base with and adequately acknowledge if not reflect this enormous literature so very much marked by diversity of interpretation and assessment. Gardiner Means dealt with many of the most fundamental topics in major fields in mid- and late-twentieth-century economics: industrial organization, microeconomics, macroeconomics, and institutional economics. And he did so in his own way. To appreciate what he had to say and his position on each topic arguably requires full consideration of the literature in each of these areas. It also requires the adoption of an interpretive perspective.

Needless to say, it would require separate volumes on each of the above fields to do justice to the substantive literature, and that is not possible here. Nonetheless we will state, and to some extent illustrate, certain conclusions concerning the varied reception given his work and the relation of his work to that of others. (We have already explored, in part, the relationship between Means's work and, for example, that of Keynes, Schumpeter, Galbraith, and others.) We also examine (in this and the following chapter) aspects of the sociology of the discipline, as one context with respect to which the place of Means in the history of economic thought has to be understood.

2. Means's Dissertation

In 1933, Gardiner Means proposed and submitted in draft form to the department of economics at Harvard University a dissertation, "The Corporate Revolution," which contained two types of materials: statistical and theoretical. The statistical material had already appeared in published journal articles and in *The Modern Corporation and Private Property*. It showed "(1) the increasing extent to which economic activity is conducted under the corporate form of organization, (2) the increasing role which corporations of tremendous size have come to play, (3) the increasing dispersion of stock ownership, and finally (4) the increasing separation of ownership and control which is involved in the modern corporation" (Means 1962a, pp. 15–16). This material was accepted and comprised the official dissertation, no copy of which apparently exists.

The theoretical materials challenged "four major postulates of received economic theory—the trading character of the market, the determinacy of costs, the unity of the process of real saving, and the efficacy of the profit motive," and argued the necessity of replacing them with themes that contradicted the original four: "(1) the administrative character of the market, (2) the indeterminacy of costs, (3) the duality of the process of saving, and finally

(4) the possible ineffectiveness of 'profits' as a motivating force'' (Means 1962a, p. 16). This material was rejected by his dissertation committee and excluded from the final dissertation.

Strangely, the account published in *Summaries of Ph.D. Theses—1933*, Harvard University, contained the summary of both the included and the excluded material, and was subsequently published by Means, from which the foregoing has been quoted (Means 1962a, pp. 15–19).[48] It became Means's view, and that of his wife, Caroline Ware, that the theoretical chapters were rejected because of the challenge they posed to received economic theory.[49] This had a chilling effect, needless to say, on Means's attitude toward his professional academic economist colleagues—an attitude which was largely reciprocated by mainstream economists, who either could not fathom or would not accept his ideas.

In what is apparently his only published comment on this episode, Means called it ''disappointing'':

> My thesis committee did not like my ''theoretical implications.'' They said they would accept the statistical section alone as my thesis, but not the theoretical section unless it was thoroughly revised. I dropped the section on theory. Yet, these implications are today widely accepted. I have always attributed this rebuff, not to the quality of my theoretical analysis, but to the impervious character of an established paradigm. (Means 1975, p. 153)

This episode, knowledge of which we have from only one side, suggests, and perhaps prefigures, aspects of the subsequent reception given to Means's writings. These center on the roles of paradigm, ideology, and, inter alia, the complexity of the problems on which he chose to work, including their susceptibility to variable specification and modeling, as well as related vagaries of data collection and manipulation. Of interest also is the acceptance of the statistical chapters and the rejection of the theoretical ones: some of the subsequent criticism was directed at his theory, and some at his empirical work. For some critics, his theory did not accord with their paradigm; for others, perhaps some of the same persons, his empirical work did not square with either their theory (or their paradigm) or their empirics (which in turn were developed on the basis of their paradigm-based theory). For some observers Means was a theoretician; for others, he was a statistician. Over the years Means (sometimes but not always along with Berle) has been deemed a major social and economic theorist. He also has been called one of the foremost innovative statisticians of his period.[50] But his (their) work as theorist and/or statistician has also been totally repudiated by others.

3. Facts, Paradigms, Ideology, and Discourse

Wiles (1987, p. 30) has sensibly and accurately written that "the full-cost principle in particular, and administered prices in general, seem to be methodologically offensive to orthodox economic theory. No facts should be that." Keyserling (1987, p. 421) has asserted, apropos of the "prevalent economic and legal thinking" at the time of *The Modern Corporation and Private Property* that "Berle and Means *proved* that this was not how the economy actually worked."

Now, we who in fact agree with the major themes of Berle and Means and with Means's general portrayal of how the economy is structured and operates must nonetheless affirm that what they did was not simply a matter of pure "facts," and that Berle and Means "proved" no such thing. What they did was to interpret reality in terms of a certain paradigm, to interpret on the basis of rather than prove that paradigm, and to identify facts in the context that it provided. The orthodox neoclassical version of the economy, whether or not in its Chicago version, is but one alternative paradigm, one more consistent with certain traditional values and the dominant ideology and the predominant school of thought. Both are modes of discourse. Both attempt to define reality and provide a basis for policy, and on the basis of each attempt the world is in part made and remade. But neither are a matter of facts which have some ostensibly independent, transcendent existence. An individual economist's adoption of either paradigm is a matter of fundamental preconceptions influenced by political and economic ideology, professional training, peer group identification, and so on, not a matter of rigorous scientific proof, the canons and conventions of professional practice notwithstanding.[51]

The ideological and paradigm-driven nature of some of the treatments given Means's work, coupled with the predominance of paradigm-specific hierarchical structures within the discipline, helps explain some of the negative views given certain of Means's ideas, for example, the work by George Stigler critical of administered pricing and price inflexibility. It remains true, however, that the basic topics are capable of variable empirical formulation and testing, such that any substantive conclusion, including Means's own, is necessarily specific to paradigm, supplemental-concept, statistical or econometric technique, and data manipulation usages. Still, for many economists and others, especially in business and in the conservative ideologically oriented institutes often supported by business, Means and his work were anathema because he seemed to challenge their conception of what business and the market were all about. This was especially true of those who understood and rationalized the market in individualist terms.

4. Already and Newly Established Fields

Means's work was seminal in certain respects, but in some areas he was working in fields with literatures that were already established, recognized, and more or less well defined. For example, in Berle's preface to their 1932 volume, William Z. Ripley was acknowledged as "having pioneered" the area (Berle and Means 1932, p. ix). Means helped generate and also helped reinforce areas of study which became more or less important in the discipline (and in related fields, such as management theory). In many areas, for many economists, albeit not for all, Means was a name to be reckoned with, eventually at least an elder statesman, someone who had contributed to the world view within which the field developed.

This was especially true in regard to the enormous success of *The Modern Corporation and Private Property*, a book which in a certain sense had a life independent of its authors. This was also true of the theory of administered pricing, for example, in relation to the theory of target return pricing and Eichner's work on markup pricing, as well as all aspects of Post Keynesian economics.

The areas of study alluded to in the preceding paragraph include the following: the corporation; the corporate system; political economy; administered pricing; price flexibility and inflexibility; the price mechanism; disequilibrium; fix-price markets; markup and target return pricing; the theory of markets; inflation; unemployment; saving-investment theory; the theory of the firm; managerial ideology; managerial strategic planning; corporate financial policy; predatory pricing and other exclusionary tactics; risk management; definitions of "competition"; the political power of corporations; the privileged status of business; industrial concentration; the dispersion of stock ownership; the separation of ownership and control; market structure; pricing theories; stagflation; the theory and institution of private property; managerial behavior theories; and the nature of rational behavior, profit maximization, and alternative goals.

Means's work did not always enter into all developments in these areas. In each area his work, approach, and/or formulation is but one among many and not utilized by all researchers. Still it is obviously impossible to trace here the place of Means and his ideas in regard to each of these fields and topics. The substantive literatures are enormous, the interpretive requirements are even greater, and both are subject to selective perception.

5. Aspects of Filtration

Both the reception given to Means's work and the status accorded to him in the discipline were quite complex and diverse. Much depended and continues to depend on the perspectives of those evaluating him and his work. Means's mixed reception and status depends on considerations and factors arising as much from the social location, paradigm, and beliefs of his evaluators as from his work itself. This involves in part the existence of nonoverlapping citation groups and in part rival insider and outsider groups, both of which are due to the conflict of schools within economics.

Mechanisms exist—such as journal peer review processes,[52] graduate student reading lists, etc.[53]—which filter out, sanitize, or marginalize, heterodox and radical ideas. What happens to Means's reputation in the future, as has happened in the past, will depend heavily upon (1) the status of institutional and Post Keynesian economics within the discipline, (2) the internal development of each of those fields, (3) the status and development of industrial organization (especially with regard to what business practices are taken as given, and the definition of competition used), and (4) the perspective from which and breadth with which future histories of economic thought are written. All of these factors will themselves be heavily influenced by the development of the core of microeconomic and macroeconomic theory, what diversions from the core become acceptable within the mainstream, and the reading and citation practices of economists—which historically have not tended to be very extensive outside of conventional in-groups.

Certain topics, themes, and/or aspects of Means's work have already been filtered out of the mainstream neoclassical literature. In some cases, they never were accepted within the mainstream to be eventually excluded. In other cases, somewhat compatible or at least analogous ideas have emerged, often with negligible attention to Means's work. (It is certainly not expected that any development in any field would necessarily touch base with all relevant past work.) Some of his ideas have been more or less accepted in the mainstream but in a neoclassicized form, such as fix-price models (though it is unlikely that Means's formulation constituted the source; more likely, his was part of the panorama of relevant work).

Much of his work has been ignored by theorists, in part because they perceived it as nontheoretical when in fact it was both empirical and theoretical, though his theorizing involved a very different paradigm of the economy from the one generally assumed. What constituted "economic theory" depended on one's subjective preferences and identification. Moreover, this was an issue not solely of theory versus empiricism, but also of theory with words versus theory with sophisticated mathematics (which subsequently became an issue of mathematical formalism versus substantive economic content).

It is not always possible to distinguish unequivocally when an idea has been filtered out of neoclassical economics from when it has been absorbed within neoclassical economics. Is the idea to be comprehended in terms of its non-neoclassical formulation or its neoclassicized construction? Any answer to the question of the status of Means's work in relation to neoclassical economics depends, in part, on one's answers to these questions.

Frederic Lee (1984) has argued, among other things, that the full-cost principle (FCP) "has undergone continual theoretical development," that "it has been absorbed into the post-Keynesian paradigm as part of the theoretical foundation of its price theory," and that while its "early developers . . . saw it as a broad and sustained attack on marginalism, a view initially accepted by many orthodox economists[,] . . . by the mid-1950s, the principle was viewed as being completely compatible with neo-classical price theory in general and marginalism in particular" (p. 233). In part, this neoclassicization took the form of a "rationalization . . . in which the mark-up was interpreted in terms of price elasticity of demand," with the result that "subsequent professional discussions . . . assumed without question the marginalist interpretation and thus viewed it as marginalism in a different language" (p. 236). Also, whereas "domestic non-neoclassical (or non-marginalist) developments of the FCP were either severely criticized or ignored[,] . . . 'foreign' interpretations of the FCP were blocked from entering the US" (p. 237). Thus, whereas P. W. S. Andrews's and Paolo Sylos-Labini's work, which presented the FCP "in a positive and non-marginalist manner," have been largely ignored in the United States, Modigliani's "neo-classical/marginalist interpretation of the FCP remained unchallenged'' (p. 238). Moreover, ''with non-neoclassical (non-marginalist) interpretations of the FCP excluded from the domain of economic knowledge, many additional arguments supporting the consistency between the FCP and neo-classical price theory were developed'' (p. 238, citing work by W. J. Baumol and R. Marris). In this manner, then, Means's work has been absorbed but neoclassicized within the mainstream—as has happened to others, including Chamberlin and Robinson themselves.

None of this has hampered the neo-Walrasian research program or story telling. Though Means (letter to John Blair, undated, p. 2) believed that administered pricing precluded the Walrasian analysis, that approach has come to coexist with, even dominate, the neoclassicized FCP analysis, just as the competitive model has not been replaced by the theories of Chamberlin, Robinson, or, for that matter, Means or Schumpeter.[54]

The FCP, like fix-price models, has been finessed through absorption and neoclassicization, coming to rest in a little corner, ignored if not denied. If emulation is a form of flattery, sincere or not, absorption, albeit with neoclassicized transformation, is a form of acknowledgement, passive but also both flattering and disappointing.

What Lee affirms with regard to the FCP, or administered pricing, is true of what Means had to say about the firm in relation to the market. Means could not have rendered his view in such marginalist terms as Coase (1988, p. 55): ''The question always is, Will it pay to bring an extra exchange transaction under the organizing authority? At the margin, the costs of organizing within the firm will be equal either to the costs of organizing in another firm or to the costs involved in leaving the transaction to be 'organized' by the price mechanism.'' Means's thesis regarding the separation of ownership and control was similarly absorbed by the mainstream. See the literature on markets for control and management as well as products (for example, Wolfson 1984, chapter 5). In such ways, ideas that are otherwise radical (vis-à-vis neoclassical theory and/or the dominant economic ideology) are rendered safe, intentionally or otherwise.[55] What is at first (and in some quarters always) denied is sometimes later accepted in a more or less sterilized form—or a form that includes acceptable ideological premises, in which the radical nuances have been finessed.

One aspect of Means's work which clearly has not been absorbed is his distinctive attempt to understand the formation of the firm's objective function. Those writers, essentially neoclassical, such as Oliver Williamson, who have worked on the firm, have generally presumed the existence of a single objective function for it, generally profit maximization. For Means explicitly (and for Williamson and others, only implicitly at best), the content of the firm's objective function—what actually, substantively constitutes maximizing behavior—is never clear but must be worked out.

By the same token, the formation of the firm's objective function is one facet of a larger subject which has developed enormously since Means's early work, and was largely ignored, certainly not written about, by Means. We have witnessed the multifaceted opening up of the corporate black box during the last thirty or so years. Some of this has stemmed from the application of game theory and other forms of decision theory; some from the application of behavioral psychology to management; some from the so-called "new" institutionalist work of Coase and Williamson; and some by business and economic historians. Contributions have been made by certain lines of work within the economics of industrial organization and macroeconomics and, of course, schools such as institutional and Post Keynesian economics. We now know much more about how corporations operate than was known during Means's early years, though precious little compared to what needs to be known. What is clear is that Means's work contributed to the education of diverse intellects which led them to study the corporation and its operations and policies—and that Means continued to work along the lines which interested him and which he considered important.

In the field of administered pricing alone there is an enormous literature. Some work reinforces, some amplifies, some qualifies, some contradicts, and some is irrelevant to or simply different from that of Means. Among the other prominent early writers were Jules Backman, W. H. Hamilton, A. D. H. Kaplan, E. G. Nourse, P. W. S. Andrews, and Willard Thorp. Much of their work has been neglected if not filtered out of—perhaps more generally, prevented from entering—the consciousness of theoretical economists and others writing under the aegis of neo-Walrasian and other neoclassical price theory. Consideration of the ramifications of highly abstract and exceedingly hypothetical general equilibrium theory of the Walrasian and neo-Walrasian type has seemingly eclipsed all efforts to examine what actually goes on in the real-world economy.

6. "A Man of One Idea"

There is a certain irony in the reputation accorded Gardiner Means. It appears that Means is often perceived to have been a "man of one idea," namely, administered prices. In a certain sense that is correct, in the same way, for example, that Harry Gunnison Brown was perceived as a disciple of Henry George and the Single Tax. (Singleness—and therefore coherence—of vision is often lauded in those whose ideas one accepts.) But it is also a gross misrepresentation and trivialization of Means's larger body of work, centering on the corporation, the nature of private property, the corporate system, an alternative microeconomics, and Post Keynesian macroeconomics. Moreover, it is rather odd to regard Means as having been concerned only with administered prices since, while many conservative economists were preoccupied for much of the post–World War II period with inflation (even when the inflation rate was slight), Means was one of the few supposedly heterodox economists to have been centrally concerned about inflation. The difference between Means and the orthodox lies in the vastly conflicting paradigms within which they understood inflation and its genesis, and the perceived radical nature of

Means's paradigm. If administered pricing was his "one idea," it was an idea brought in service to the war against inflation—and this is correct whether Means was right or wrong in his analysis of its origins. But surely it is incorrect to identify Means solely with that one idea.

7. Recollections of Early Perceptions

Frederic Lee has received numerous interesting and insightful responses to a letter of inquiry sent to economists who were active during the administered price controversy in the 1930s, not all of which pertained exclusively to the question of administered pricing. The letters provide information on the reception of Means's work within academia, including, but not limited to, the extent to which Means's ideas were studied or at least discussed in graduate and undergraduate economics courses and in informal discussions, and the views of the letter writers themselves of Means's work. Altogether the responses constitute an interesting source of insight, though nothing hard or conclusive.

The picture that emerges from the responses is quite complex. Means's work (especially *Industrial Prices and Their Relative Inflexibility* and *The Structure of the American Economy*) was more or less widely read and discussed. The controversy was included in some undergraduate and graduate programs but not in all. It was included, for example, in courses at Catholic University and Harvard, the latter course taught by Edward Mason (Martin E. Schirber, 11 December 1987, who also writes that "the doctrine of administered prices was quite widely discussed in undergrad and graduate levels"). But because it was not consonant with received theory, it could not readily be absorbed without affirming an anomaly. "Normal science" (in Kuhn's terminology) rejects or marginalizes anomalous ideas: it can hardly react in any other way without endangering its hard core (in the sense of Lakatos) and the equanimity of its practitioners.

Frank J. Kottke (15 September 1987) felt that "in the late thirties economists had relatively little data at their disposal; still, his [Means's] specification of the problem was crude and invited much pointless criticism.'' Kottke also noted that ''academic economists tend to be narrow specialists.''

Tibor Scitovsky (2 October 1987) has the impression ''that faculties were certainly aware of Means's work, considered it interesting and worth reading but probably didn't know how to react to it.'' Scitovsky notes that the case (''by far the most important'') of ''price setting by someone with a bargaining advantage on one side of the market . . . was I think first drawn attention to by Gardiner Means; although the profession adopted my terminology (price maker) rather than Means's. He failed, of course, to explain why and under what circumstances an administrator is able to set prices.'' The reader will note three aspects of the situation represented in Scitovsky's account: difficulty in knowing how to react; partial adoption of a neoclassicized version; and the desire for further elaboration. The first of these is characteristic of ''normal science''; the second, of diversity and of filtration and transformation; and the third, suggestive of both the lack of support Means had with which to provide the further elaboration and the fact that others failed to jump on the bandwagon and work out his ideas.

Margaret S. Gordon wrote of her husband, Robert Aaron Gordon, that he ''was not exactly a believer in Means' administered price doctrine, but was extremely skeptical that the formal marginalism that characterized neoclassical theory could be useful in the light of the uncertainty that prevails in the complex environment in which business decisions have to be made.'' Gordon was, of course, a major investigator of business leadership in the large corporations.

Alfred Kahn (8 September 1987), a contributor to Means (1975), wrote that Means's work ''had a very strong influence'' on him and ''the excitement (no doubt partially misplaced) engendered'' by his reading *Industrial Prices and Their Relative Inflexibility* ''played a large role in attracting'' him into economics. He continues "to think that the controversy was and is important, even though the various commentaries on the Means hypothesis have properly made it seem somewhat less earth-shaking than it seemed at the time." Kahn points to related work by Richard Ruggles and to the influence of Means on work by Paolo Sylos-Labini.

Ralph C. Hon (8 September 1987) refers to notes from a conversation with C. P. Spruil of the University of North Carolina in 1935 in which the latter is recorded as saying that "Means' statement on the relative inflexibility of industrial prices is the greatest contribution to economic theory during the past 25 years." One wonders if the term "theory" was intended to encompass all of economic analysis, both theoretical and inductive, or only the former.

Raymond J. Saulnier (5 October 1987) believes that "depression in the 1930s, when many prices and wage rates remained unchanged in the face of collapsing demand, gave a relevance to what Means was saying that would not otherwise have been there." At Columbia College and Barnard College, writes Saulnier, "the administered pricing debate was very much a part of what we were discussing. It was so also in the graduate faculty, but there was more attention there to the work on imperfect competition (Joan Robinson) and monopolistic competition (Edward Chamberlin) that competed for the attention of those of us interested in formal theory. Partly because his work was more 'institutional' than the Cambridge and Harvard writers, and perhaps less 'elegant' in form, I think it is fair to say that Means was more on the periphery than at the center of the academic debates on price theory at the time." This suggests that economists can only handle so many new ideas at a time, that formal theory is per se attractive, and that the development of theory is heavily influenced by sociological considerations such as status as well as by the congruence of the new ideas with, or utility in further developing, the received paradigm.[56]

Richard Goode (8 September 1987) worked with Means (and Gerhard Colm) at the Fiscal Division of the Bureau of the Budget in 1941 and became "well acquainted" with Means's work. Goode notes that "Means was optimistic about the productive capacity of the American economy . . . '' and that ''Means had an original mind and preferred to work matters out for himself and in conversation rather than by extensive reading.'' This latter reinforces the sense that Means was something of a loner, an outsider in part by choice if not also as a result of the treatment accorded him by the mainstream.

Charles Hession (1 September 1987) reports that his doctoral dissertation on the metal container industry convinced him ''that administered prices were a reality.'' He also thinks that ''George Stigler's essay on Rigid Prices was quite important in casting doubt on Means' thesis, but I do not think that it altogether demolished it.''

John B. McFerrin (4 September 1987) reports that in 1936, Carl Snyder, then a visiting professor at the University of North Carolina, thought that the idea of administered prices ''had no merit.''

Robert W. Harbeson (5 September 1987) recollects that the subject of administered prices ''received a moderate amount of attention but did not by any means occupy the center of the stage'' and suggests that this was in part due to ''data limitations and relatively undeveloped state of oligopoly theory and econometric analysis at that time.''

Earl Rolph (undated) reports that ''the topic [of administered prices] was not a 'burning issue' '' at Berkeley ''nor was it of much interest to me'' and that ''the controversy about the topic, if more than 'hot air' [a phrase used in Lee's letter of inquiry], was not of much use in understanding pricing behavior in the American economy in my opinion.'' Rolph adds that Berle and Means was used as one text in an undergraduate course on industrial organization there in 1937–1938.

Robert R. Nathan (16 December 1987) has the ''strong impression that Gardiner Means made a significant contribution to the field of price competition and to its relationship to concentration of economic power.''

William F. Kennedy (7 September 1987) reports Walter Mead's view to be that ''the controversy was important, but that the Means thesis was effectively controverted by the work of George Stigler and others.'' Kennedy himself believes that ''Means made an important contribution; it was original and had an impact on economics.'' He attributes the eclipse of ''the work of Means and other institutionalists'' to the revival of ''theory'' that resulted from the work of Keynes. It may well be that anyone then writing in a manner not readily perceived to be congruent with the received paradigm and corpus of theory was assigned to the class of institutionalists. In the case of Means, this was not wrong.

Gardner Ackley (26 September 1987) reports that in the 1930s he ''read at least some of Means' work.'' He ''followed the Administered-Price controversy, with considerable interest. A few of my associates did, too; but my hunch (more than my memory) is that most of the 'deep thinkers', the well-known names, paid less attention—perhaps very little attention—to it. After all, the Administered-Price approach did criticize—and even contradict—ideas which were fundamental to ways that we all had been used to, had often taught, and in some cases that we had developed or extended. Graduate students and younger faculty had less of an investment in the established truth, and were more likely to be interested and tempted.'' He thinks that ''most intellectually . . . [active] economists dipped into it, and talked about it—whether or not they sympathized with it. Some of us undoubtedly referred to it in our teaching.'' However, it was ''the Keynesian apostasy'' which attracted many economists, and ''the two revolutions were not related; either *historically* or intellectually. But the connections were and are not obvious.'' This account is obviously pregnant with ideas either already discussed or to be raised below.

Moses Abramovitz (21 July 1987) responded that the controversy ''was certainly regarded'' as important and that ''even those who disagreed strongly with Means took his views seriously.'' He also says that the doctrine and the controversy ''certainly was a subject in graduate classes and seminars.'' Abramovitz reports that ''Milton Friedman . . . thought Means' views tended strongly in the direction of government control of prices—a 'fascist' policy, perhaps by analogy with what Hjalmar Schacht was doing in Germany.'' Means, as we have noted, had quite the opposite view.

Weir M. Brown (7 August 1987) reports that while ''reference was made to the views of Means, much more attention was given the books'' by Chamberlin and Robinson. His own ''not-too-considered reaction at that time was that Means's ideas represented one more attempt, based on some price and production data drawn from the depression years, to diagnose some factors contributing to that crisis and, of course, to offer a planned solution.'' He adds that ''neither Robinson nor Chamberlin lists Means in their bibliographies—not even in the nearly 1500 titles listed in Chamberlin's 1960 edition.'' The last point is suggestive with regard to the existence of citation groups.

Dudley Dillard (18 August 1987) wrote Lee that ''the work of Gardiner Means on administered prices was known to all faculty and students in the late thirties at Berkeley'' and that ''in courses in general economic theory, inflexible prices was always a factor to be contended with,'' though there was more focus on Chamberlin's work. ''On the Berkeley faculty my impression is that both liberal and conservative members more or less accepted administered prices as a fact of the American economy.'' This remembrance certainly differs from others.

Wolfgang F. Stolper (6 October 1987) reports two interesting things. First, as a graduate student, instructor, and tutor at Harvard in the late 1930s, ''I read then as did everyone else of my fellow students Berle and Means's famous book. As far as I recall after five decades, we were all impressed and discussed it in great detail, particularly in its relevance to standard competitive price theory.'' Second, as a teacher in the introductory course, ''we were a bunch of young Turks, introducing such radical ideas as marginal cost = marginal revenue—yes, this was once great news thought fit only for advanced graduate students. . . .'' But, he notes, administered pricing was also covered.

Donald L. Kemmerer's response (12 October 1987) is noteworthy for his reference to the administered pricing controversy as a matter not of economic history but of economic theory.

C. Lowell Harriss (11 October 1987) reports that "it is my admittedly imprecise recollection that for a time Means' conclusions about administered prices received rather wide acceptance. I believe that the thesis was often cited as one explanation for unemployment continuing and the slowness of recovery." While he was a graduate student at Chicago during 1936–1938, "the inflexibility of wage rates in the unionized sectors was cited. I do not recall that Means put emphasis on wages as administered prices, but we did hear of the relationship to quantity of employment." He had earlier learned from Arthur Robert Burns at Columbia about price inflexibility "and why changes were less frequent than changes in underlying conditions might seem to justify" in the steel industry. The reader will note, inter alia, that for some economists wage inflexibility due to unionization was more readily comprehensible than commodity price inflexibility due to the Berle-Means analysis of the corporation, at least in part because of ideology, inasmuch as unions could be viewed as an intrusion into otherwise competitive markets.

Abram Bergson (18 July 1987) recalls "being much impressed as a graduate student by some of Means's work, particularly the contrast he drew between 'administered' and other prices in respect of their response to the Great Depression. I can report, too, that in Cambridge his work was of wide interest among students and faculty at the time."

Albert Gailord Hart (9 September 1987; typographical errors corrected) reports that at Chicago "Henry Simons (the real leader of the real Chicago School) persuaded the Chicago group that the free competitive market was something we didn't have but should strive toward. I can't remember that Means was discussed in this connection, though we did give weight to the famous Berle/Means thesis." Undergraduate teaching used certain exercises "which contrasted the results of free competitive markets and those of a *cartel*. The cartel price was pictured as 'administered'. I can't remember that students ever heard of Means in this connection.'' Hart also reports that at the Committee for Economic Development Means ''played the role of well-received gadfly,'' that he persuaded his colleagues to support the extension of war-time price controls until mid-1947 (which did not happen), and that he ''announced himself to be a protectionist.'' The irony of Simons's view of the status of the free competitive market is at least noteworthy.

Alfred H. Bornemann (22 July 1987) reports that Lewis H. Haney taught the NYU theory course without mentioning Means's material, but that *Economic Behavior* (Atkins et al. 1931, 1939) did examine ''the myriad features of price-making,'' and the revised edition ''did contain the term administered prices, as well as references to'' Means's principal works. Bornemann thinks that ''everyone in economics was at least generally aware'' of Means's work ''and students were also expected to be.'' He, too, says that Chamberlin's work was ''talked about'' more ''and of course the rage was getting to be macro, and Keynes and Hansen.'' If this report is at all modally representative, Means was then in fact part of the economics mainstream, though apparently not of pure theory.

John Dean Gaffey (3 September 1987) wrote to Lee that ''the ideas of price leadership and the theory of oligopoly as developed by Profs. Arthur R. Burns, Joe Bain, Mason, Wilcox, Pegrum and others was related to that of Means and owed quite a lot to him.'' This speaks loudly of an important but perhaps not central place for Means in the prewar origins of industrial organization theory.

Richard A. Lester (8 September 1987) reported that ''there was considerable discussion of Berle and Means and also some of Means' writings on 'administered prices' in the Princeton economics department during the period I was teaching here from 1934–1938.''

Wilfred Malenbaum (16 September 1987) recounts that ''most of our Harvard graduate students had some exposure to Gardner [*sic*] Means. . . . He came to Littauer seminars and certainly our mentor in this area, Ed Mason, gave his themes considerable attention in seminar subjects and in classes." "Even with insights of today, I would say few of the students and faculty I knew considered Means' themes a lot of hot air. Most of us benefited from the readings and discussions. His was certainly not a breakthrough subject compared to the other breakthroughs of those prewar years."

Martin Bronfenbrenner (4 September 1987) reports that he and his colleagues did follow the administered price controversy, and the work of Temporary National Economic Committee (TNEC), "with great interest" and that he "heard nobody refer to the controversy at that time as 'a lot of hot air.' " Like one or two other respondents, he notes having used Means and Ware's (1936) book in undergraduate courses. He too reports that at Chicago "Henry Simons agreed with Means that administered prices were delaying recovery and should come down. (But Simons was already more down on trade-union wages than on industrial prices.)" Referring to Means's failed attempt to secure *American Economic Review* space for an answer to Stigler, Bronfenbrenner says "I still think that on this latest resurgence of controversy, Means was more nearly right than Stigler and/or the *AER* editorial board."

Eli Ginzberg (14 September 1987) stresses that one needs "to note that economics was at loose ends in the great depression . . . which meant that any broad doctrine such as administered prices had a chance to make a splash. It was *not* viewed as 'hot air' but neither was it embraced by most economists. It was out there and neither the proponents nor the critics made much headway." He suspects "that some of the more critical economists who were unhappy about the neo-classical paradigm surely used GM and did so approvingly." Ginzberg also reports that "GM was much less of a mind than his collaborator A. A. Berle. And I do recall that Ed Mason's work finally convinced me that Means was in far over his depth." (Another writer has the impression that it was primarily among the students of John D. Black in agricultural economics at Harvard that the interest in Means's work was greatest, deriving largely from the support that his findings lent to agricultural relief programs; and that while the administered price material was included in the elementary course and, through incidence theory, in the public finance course, this was due more to the influence of Chamberlin than of Means. Eugene E. Oakes, 5 October 1987.)

Irving H. Siegel (4 December 1987) writes:

> As a novice in the 1930's, I felt that the "controversy" over Means's innovation was *both* "important" and "a lot of hot air." His attachment of the word "administered" to a phenomenon suggested by B.L.S. [Bureau of Labor Statistics] price statistics had *ideological* force. It helped to confirm the "conspiracy" theories of "New Dealers," "liberals," etc. and to arouse the "economic royalists," "bourbons," and "reactionaries" defending the "free market." I was a fence-sitter. My youth, job-hunting experience, and "class" origin inclined me to distrust untrammeled private price-setting. On the other hand, the luck of serving as a research assistant to a "social Darwinist," Prof. Willford I. King (at N.Y.U.) permitted me to detect the "hot air." Working with King on the Commonwealth Edison rate case in 1934–36, I learned that many large companies . . . kept constant public price lists but gave substantial discounts. . . . Such companies surely did not report "net" prices to B.L.S. or any other compiler.

Moreover, "Means ranked higher in Prof. Corwin Edwards's course in 'Industrial [O]rganization' than in Professor Mills's seminars in 'Economic Processes.' " The implication of the political significance of ostensibly positive ideas is evident.

Samuel P. Hayes (31 August 1987) writes that "although I can't appraise Means's impact on theoretical thinking, it is clear that a lot of empirical research on prices was going on in the thirties, and his views were certainly important in framing the research questions investigated."

Chelcie C. Bosland (31 July 1987) says that "the faculty at Brown gave about typical attention to the question of corporate concentration and 'administered' prices when it was popular in the depression era of the 1930's and 1940's. It was an important controversy, but hardly an all-consuming one." She notes her early "doubts about the validity of his conclusions. They seemed to be overly simplistic and inadequate to measure the many forces that determine price behavior. But he made a useful contribution by raising a question that led others to make significant research studies." She also writes, "perhaps I am wrong, but I have felt that Means was more a reformer or crusader than an objective economist, partly because of his government associations. But he did pose questions that called for answers."

8. The Status of Means's Work

We come now to the truly herculean if not impossible task of providing some understanding of the treatment of Means in the relevant literature. This literature, as indicated above, is truly enormous. The treatment of Berle and Means and of Means alone varies with the paradigm, ideology, approaches to model building and data massage, and personal idiosyncrasy or selective perception of individual writers. That this is true also of attempts to assess reception and status is suggested by both this volume itself and the papers given at the Hoover Institution conference on the fiftieth anniversary of *The Modern Corporation and Private Property* (Moore et al. 1983). Most of the contributors to that conference volume were antagonistic to the book's argument. But what more powerful recognition could there be of the status of the book, even greater than the begrudging tribute rendered by the fact of the conference itself, than (1) the recounting by Moore (1983, p. 235) that the Social Science Citation Index reports that for 1981 the citations to Berle and Means were exceeded in number only by other classic works by Keynes, Von Neumann, Schumpeter, Hicks, and Pigou, and (2) Stigler and Friedland's (1983, p. 237) statement that "there are not many books fifty years old whose central argument is identified for modern economists simply by naming the work, but Berle and Means's *The Modern Corporation and Private Property* is surely one."

The principal argument of this section is that the treatment accorded Means in the relevant literature is exceedingly heterogeneous and reflects the heterogeneity of economics and of the other fields to which his work relates. The same is true of several of the subjects with which Means is associated, subjects which are not of interest to many mainstream economists, such as administered pricing in macroeconomic theory.

We shall document this argument at some length by constructing several mosaics based on random explorations into the literatures of relevant fields in economics. This approach, it should be said, does not do justice to at least five things. First, it does not substantiate the enormous status of Berle and Means in fields outside of economics, such as law and political science. Second, it does not substantiate the failure to treat Means's work in some leading books in fields in which other leading books do treat his work. Third, it does not deal at all with the enormous empirical literature ostensibly testing Meansian themes on concentration, administered pricing, and administered inflation. Fourth, it ignores the literature of business management which studies and/or teaches how firms set prices and pursue goals, writings in which Means's work typically does not enter, but which substantiate and illuminate some of his arguments. Fifth, it does not do complete justice to the literature in which Means's ideas are criticized. The general rule, apropos of the last matter, is that for anything affirmative said about a Meansian argument there is something negative also said about it—a situation that results from the fact that there are conflicting schools of thought, paradigms, ideologies, modes of modeling, and data massage. One example of this is the diametrically opposed pictures and conclusions given on administered pricing by Greer (1980, chapter 11) and Martin (1988, chapter 14).

(a) A General Mosaic

If the treatment rendered Means within mainstream, orthodox neoclassical economics is the evaluative base, then Means is not a very important figure. If the interests and ideas of institutional and Post Keynesian economists, and many political scientists, law professors, and sociologists are considered, Means is a much more important figure. The arguable neoclassical neglect and/or rejection of Means's ideas should not obscure the enormous success of *The Modern Corporation and Private Property*. This work is of truly classic and seminal importance in the multidisciplinary literature dealing with the corporation and private property—not that all writers agree with everything said by the authors; far from it. Studies in all relevant disciplines on these topics are more sophisticated because of the work of Berle and Means, not the least law and even economics, and the treatment given the book reflects this situation. This is the case, notwithstanding the fact that microeconomic and macroeconomic theory, as well as the microeconomic foundations of economics, have largely followed neo-Walrasian paths which are extremely uncongenial to Means's ideas. Yet even in those fields, even outside of Post Keynesian economics, where Means's reputation is the highest, not all work is neo-Walrasian.

Consider, first, a current attempt by Benjamin Friedman (1988) to articulate "Harvard's world view." He argues that it "includes central roles of aggregate demand, sticky prices and wages, slow-moving equilibrium process" and so on (pp. 47, 52). The "lessons of recent years" are said to "have reinforced the understanding that . . . the ability of many of the modern economy's markets to move quickly to positions of supply-determined equilibrium are themselves often highly limited." This is "because movements in market prices are often limited, and because the feasible economic responses of both individuals and institutions to what movements in market prices do occur are also limited" (p. 52). This does not exactly describe administered prices but it does affirm the core of what we argue that Means had to say about the price adjustment process. Gardiner C. Means seems to have no place in Friedman's account (historical or analytical) but his presence pervades the story like Banquo's ghost. Harvard may not be Post Keynesian, but it is also not neo-Walrasian. Friedman's is a story, within the neoclassical mainstream (unless Harvard be read out of that mainstream), radically different from Chicago, dominated as that school is by quantity theory, rational expectations, new classical economics, and supply-side economics—though regarding the last, Friedman acknowledges the presence and force of Martin Feinstein.

Consider also Rodney Peterson's brief survey (in W. C. Peterson 1988b, pp. 9–12) of the major contributions to the nonmainstream neoclassical analysis of power, including Abba Lerner, Kurt Rothchild, Andreas Papandreau, Joe Bain, and Norman Collins and Lee Preston. These all follow the maximization hypothesis and devote little or no attention to how firm management comes to comprehend and determine the substance of profit maximization, but market power is present, in one form or another. In this same volume, John Munkirs (1988) relates Means's work in part to Chamberlin's and Robinson's arguments about the micro and macro problems consequent on "*widespread* market power," such as "idle capacity, allocative and X-inefficiency, high unemployment, monopoly prices, deadweight welfare loss, inflation, wage exploitation, increases in wealth and income maldistribution, etc." (p. 34). For all of Chamberlin's evident orthodoxy, his ideas opened up quite heterodox doors within the nonhomogeneous mainstream, and these were doors through which Means had passed, often before Chamberlin.

Going back earlier, one reads in Drucker's (1946, pp. 5, 6–7) influential volume on the concept of the corporation:

> The large industrial unit has become our representative social actuality; and its social organization, the large corporation in this country, our representative social institution. In other words, Big Business is the general condition of modern industrial society irrespective of the forms of social organization or the political beliefs adopted in particular countries. . . . What is essential in a society is . . . not the static mass but the dynamic element; not the multitude of facts but the symbol through which the facts are organized in a social pattern; not, in other words, the average but the representative. And this, in our society today, is the large corporation.

The modern corporation is more than a simple profit maximizing economic actor. Mund and Wolf (1971), in their textbook on industrial organization, write thus:

> It is now generally recognized that the power of control, which traditionally resided in business owners, has become concentrated in large corporations in the hands of a relatively few managers—paid professionals. These few are largely able to perpetuate and replace themselves in office by controlling the proxy system, an arrangement whereby management secures the votes of absentee stockholders for its use in electing the board of directors. Professor Berle has observed that in the large corporations of today the election of directors by stockholders has become "a ritual rather than a reality." The few in control no longer depend upon property ownership for their power or authority. Instead they are virtually immune from effective stockholder control. Control is beyond property. If stockholders do not like corporate policies, they have the alternative of selling their shares. (p. 444)

R. A. Gordon (1945, p. 350), writing in a general context of professionalized leadership in the large corporation, and more specifically about ways of making corporate boards of directors more independent of management, defends such efforts against the charge that such changes would revolutionize the property rights of stockholders. He says, citing Berle and Means, that "the real revolution has already largely taken place; the great majority of stockholders have [*sic*] been deprived of control of their property through the diffusion of ownership and the growth in the power of management."

W. H. Ferry (1964, p. 111, quoting Means 1964, p. 67) argues that "when Gardiner Means observes that 'the modern corporation has undermined the preconceptions of classical economic theory as effectively as the quantum undermined classical physics at the beginning of the twentieth century,' he is not indicting the corporation but prescribing one of the important intellectual tasks of our time." The reader will observe two points: affirmation of Means's conservative attitude toward the corporation; and criticism of the methodological and normative individualism of economic theory in the face of an actual economy of managerialism.

F. M. Scherer's (1971) textbook on industrial organization, which centers on market structure and its consequences for economic performance, attempts to interpret the then-existing evidence and concludes in part as follows:

> Clearly, the links between market concentration, wage behavior, and the trend of prices over time are not simple. A great deal remains to be learned. In view of the residual uncertainties, it is difficult to reach confident generalizations concerning the administered price inflation thesis. Certainly it involves more than mere sound and fury. On both *a priori* and empirical grounds, there is reason to believe that wages and prices in concentrated industries are relatively inflexible downward, even when business conditions turn sour. During periods of sustained, more or less normal prosperity, producers with market power show an above-average proclivity to yield generous wage concessions. These are passed along to consumers through higher prices, and they form a pattern to be matched in competitive markets when demand conditions permit. This combination of prices rigid downward but flexible upward can cause ratchet-effect inflation even when aggregate demand is in balance with supply. On the other hand, monopolistic and oligopolistic sellers appear to display some short-run price restraint and perhaps also wage restraint during booms. What we do not know is the exact dynamics and the net secular effect of these patterns, and therefore we cannot reach a balanced assessment of how serious the administered price inflation problem is. The author's personal interpretation is that the price-setting and wage bargaining practices of concentrated industries do make it more difficult to maintain overall price stability and full employment simultaneously, but that administered price inflationary stimuli have been of modest importance compared to more traditional influences such as the pull of demand in a superheated economy. (p. 303; see also pp. 322–23)

It is not clear that Gardiner Means actually claimed more than this.

Ten years earlier, M. E. Dimock (1961) had written about the Kefauver investigation of administered prices:

> Professional opinion on this issue of so-called sticky prices is sharply divided. Professor Donald Dewey, reviewing the hearings, remarked that "the net effect . . . is to make one depressed with the state of economics as a profession," whereas Gardiner Means, who has studied administered prices more than any other economist, believes that "this phenomenon requires the rebuilding of practically all economic theory except that of perfect competition." (p. 91)

One thing is certain: for all the efforts to refute or discredit Means's arguments, for all the failure to discuss his arguments when quite conceivably they could and should have been discussed, Means has been a major if erratically treated figure in economics.

(b) Random Surveys of Several Fields within Economics

(i) Keynes and Keynesian Economics

Our survey of the literature on Keynes and Keynesian macroeconomics suggests that the direct impact, or at least specific treatment, of Means has been negligible. Means is evidently not considered a major figure and certainly he does not receive the attention given to others. He was not a member of the citation- or in-group during the years in which mainstream Keynesian macroeconomics was developed in the 1930s and the decades after World War II. He was not much interested in the formal theoretical niceties and puzzles which came to interest many theorists, and which greatly helped to make their reputations. Means, not unlike most of those who eventually became Post Keynesians, was an outsider, treated if at all at the margin of discussion. What concerned Means evidently did not concern the mainstream theorists of macroeconomics. The saving-investment relationship and liquidity preference were more interesting topics than the flexibility of prices, which was one reason, perhaps, for the later warm reception given the neo-Walrasian approach with its presumption of flexible, market-clearing prices.

A possible explanation for the negligible impact of Means is indicated by the view that "it takes a theory to kill a theory." According to this view, as developed by Salant (1978, p. 47), "facts are not sufficient, at least not until they become overwhelming. The proponents of established theory are skillful at ignoring facts that conflict with it. You need a theoretical refutation of established theory to make acceptable a policy that flies in its face." The example Salant offers is apposite a paper by Arthur Okun:

> presenting a model with a sector in which prices are set competitively and another sector in which sellers rationally make the prices and take whatever quantities of sales of output emerge. This was essentially, a theoretical explanation of administered prices; it presented no new facts, only a theory. Gardiner Means and others have been talking about administered prices for about four decades and appear to have had very little impact on theorists, but Okun's paper, simply by giving a more satisfactory explanation of facts that had been observed for decades, seems to have advanced the subject. And I would predict that, as a result, the facts will now be taken more seriously.

This quotation warrants several comments. (1) Means's work contains not only empirical evidence but "theoretical" explanations arguably richer than Okun's. (2) "Theorists" failed to accept Means's work as a theorist—or much of Okun's, for that matter. Theorists are not the discipline's sole membership, though they enjoy a certain hierarchical status (and therefore sometimes act and are treated as if they were indeed the only members), in part owing to the profession's emphasis on sophisticated mathematical techniques. Perhaps the key point, alas, is that mathematical technique rather than economic substance has very much driven the development of theory. Means's theoretical economics might have gained better acceptance if his work had been more mathematically sophisticated in its exposition. (3) Okun's formulation is a very neoclassicized version of administered pricing, in contrast with Means's. (4) One wonders in this context what happened to all the alleged statistical refutation of Means's administered pricing "data."

(ii) Intermediate Microeconomics

Our survey of intermediate microeconomics texts, like our survey of the Keynesian literature, demonstrates complexity. Means's topics are sometimes included, other times excluded. Means's arguments are sometimes affirmed, other times rejected, and still other times ignored.

Carter and Snavely (1961, pp. 231–232), for example, basing their findings on "numerous studies," claim that "there is no question concerning the widespread use of this [markup] pricing technique."

Awh (1976, p. 238), citing Lanzillotti (1958), writes that the most typical pricing objectives given in interviews by the managers of twenty large corporations were (1) achieving a target rate of return on investment, that is markup pricing; (2) stabilizing price and margin; (3) realizing a target market share; and (4) meeting or preventing price competition.

Sher and Pinola (1981, p. 706) instruct the student that markup pricing is "the rule rather than the exception in our economic system."

Carroll (1983, pp. 486–488) examines the Means-Stigler controversy over the existence of administered prices, in which each uses the same data but reaches opposite conclusions. Carroll concludes that "the rigid price prediction has not so much been disproved as defamed" (p. 488). While some writers say that the administered price will only correspond to the profit-maximizing price by accident, other writers, such as Salvatore (1983, p. 269) and Varian (1987, pp. 416–418), say that firms constantly setting prices at levels inconsistent with profit maximization will fail.

Regarding the separation of ownership and control, Varian (1987, p. 323) mentions that while ownership and control are often separated in the corporation, managers are likely to choose those actions that are in the interests of the owners. For Means, of course, such a view was highly presumptive (based on unproven assumptions) and misleading.

Scott (1973, p. 256) says that there is "no clear answer" to the questions of whether management is immune from stockholder threats or whether the implications of stockholder dissatisfaction are sufficient to get management to manage in the stockholders' interests.

Carroll (1983, pp. 502–504) considers the "managerialist school" (encompassing Galbraith, Baumol, Simon, and Cyert and March), which emphasizes that increased managerial discretion makes profit maximization an impossible goal. He holds that managers are utility maximizers and that their behavior is not likely to be consistent with profit-maximizing behavior, though tying executive compensation to the level of profits will make utility maximization more consistent with profit maximization.

According to Hartley and Tisdell (1981), three developments called into question the profit-maximizing postulate. First, evidence seemed to indicate that firms do not maximize profits. Second, the separation of ownership and control was thought to lead to managerial pursuit of self-interest rather than the interests of the owners. Third, discretionary behavior and the pursuit of managerial self-interest was seen to be more likely in imperfect markets. They maintain that the separation of ownership and control does not imply that firms do not maximize profits; that the firm's cost of production and the form of the employment contract negotiated between top management and the shareholders primarily determine the extent to which firms maximize profits; and that several forces may act to correct managerial pursuit of its own ends, such as the appearance of rivals from within or without the firm and competition for managerial jobs in the presence of high perks. Assuming that ownership knows how management is acting, it will make corresponding adjustments to the contracts of the managers (pp. 172–173 and passim).

Thompson (1985, pp. 311, 314) says that "separation of ownership and control in corporations allows executives some measure of freedom to fulfill personal goals," and concludes that firms often have multiple and differing goals, and they manifest Simon's satisficing rather than maximizing behavior.

Mansfield (1985) says that firms may engage in satisficing behavior rather than maximizing profits because the calculations required for profit maximization are too complicated and the available data too poor (p. 178). Although profit maximization "may be a reasonable first approximation, it seems likely that there is a certain amount of slack in most firms, in the sense that costs are not pushed down to the minimum" (p. 179). According to Mansfield, when the choice is between serving its own interests and those of the owners, management is likely to choose its own interests. The separation of ownership and control in large corporations is important here, says Mansfield, because owners usually have little detailed knowledge of the firm's operations. Mansfield cites other theories of managerial goals but concludes that profit maximization remains the standard assumption in microeconomics, in part because it is a close enough approximation for many purposes (something which is alleged but not demonstrated) and in part because other theories of firm behavior require more in the way of data than does the theory of profit maximization. This view seems (1) to impugn economists' concern with the real world (they are, after all, telling a story) and (2) to raise the question of why the assumption that profit maximization defines managerial goals requires less data than other assumptions—in a discipline which does not seek to generate very much, if any, relevant data as a basis for choice. The great problem, of course, is the absence of an independent test of managerial reward at the market level and/or of the relationship between managerial interests and stockholder interests, considerations which in practice tend to be resolved by assumption dependent upon paradigm consonance.

Nicholson (1987, p. 257) paraphrases Adam Smith (1937, p. 700) as to how directors "being the managers of other people's money than of their own, it cannot well be expected that they should watch over it with the same anxious vigilance with which [owners] watch over their own."

Blair and Kenny (1987, p. 192) say that owners can tie management compensation to profits to some extent, but, owing to the existence of imperfect information, management still will not maximize profits: "only owners have the full incentive to maximize profit. . . . No one else has the proper incentive to make sure that supplies are being purchased at the lowest possible prices, . . . and that hired managers are not providing themselves with plush offices, boondoggle business trips, and so on."

Garb (1981, p. 106) cites Harvey Leibenstein's X-inefficiency as the basis for pointing out that labor and management often do not work as hard or as effectively as they can. This shirking is possible because of an incomplete contract which allows laborers and managers to interpret their own duties at least up to a certain point.

Hirschleifer (1988, p. 164) acknowledges that critics point to the separation of ownership and control to support the thesis that firms do not maximize profits, but argues that both (1) the ability of owners to sue management for damages if owners believe that their contract with management has been violated, and (2) the threat of takeover will keep management responsive to owner interests. He goes on to say that "there is no doubt that managers sometimes serve their own interests at the expense of the owners," but "for the purposes of economic analysis no alternative description of the goals of the business firm has proved to be more useful than the standard concept of the profit-maximizing firm." Means, of course, would have questioned the content of that alleged utility.

One difference among writers turns on the relative emphasis given to (1) practices and structures found in the actual economy, especially those departing from the conception of a pure competitive market, and (2) the pure logic of the market. When the latter is stressed, then inter alia, pure market adjustments generated by rational behavior overwhelm all complications.

(iii) Intermediate Macroeconomics

The principal recent mainstream macroeconomics texts typically ignore Post Keynesian economics in general and Means in particular, though he has plenty of company.

Estey (1956) reviews the reasons which might lead a firm to refrain from cutting prices in a recession and presents both Means's explanation of administered prices and Rufus Tucker's criticism. Estey concludes that "the controversy indicates that our knowledge of the significance of flexible and inflexible prices is too limited to be sure that inflexibility is increasing, or that it is caused by concentration of economic power, or that it was a substantial factor in the great reduction of output in the depression of 1929–1933" (p. 465).

Powelson (1960, p. 523) says that the monopolist or monopolistic competitor has some administrative control over price and can decide whether and when to raise it by administrative decision, but also says that "administered prices may be just as competitive as market prices, despite the fact that the latter fluctuate more often and more freely." Powelson also says that to have administered inflation you must also have demand inflation (p. 524).

Ackley (1961) contains perhaps the most extensive treatment of administered price inflation among any of the more conventional older textbooks. Ackley claims that wages and the prices of most goods and services are administered, that they are characterized by being set by the seller and maintained at the same level for a long period of time, rather than being determined by a continuous bidding process reflective of supply and demand conditions, that they largely take the form of a markup over costs, and that the markup gets cumulated through the economy (pp. 440, 449, 452–453). He identifies the need to produce a theoretical framework for analyzing inflation which assumes administered prices and wages (p. 451). Ackley acknowledges the criticism of the markup theory that says that the size of the markup reflects and changes with more fundamental supply and demand forces, operating through inventories. Ackley responds that changes in markups occur only moderately with changes in demand and that the markup hypothesis is much more useful than the market-clearing supply and demand hypothesis for explaining inflation (pp. 455–456). This, of course, is a matter of selective perception (which is not to say that it is wrong in any absolute sense). Ackley also argues that cost inflation is caused by an interaction between labor's wage-setting policies and business's price-setting policies (p. 458).

Chambers (1961, p. 536) states that "in significant segments of the economy, prices and wages are rigid in the face of deflationary influences and flexible in periods of economic expansion" and attributes this to administered pricing.

Some writers argue that administered price inflation occurs when wage increases and price markups exceed the rate of productivity growth (Chambers 1961, p. 537); others argue that administered prices proceed upward faster than costs (Shapiro 1966, p. 519). (Shapiro also notes that firms that administer prices are unlikely to change prices unless fundamental demand and supply conditions change, because their prices are already at an "equilibrium" level consistent with either profit maximization or whatever goal is set by the management.)

Vickrey (1964, p. 179) acknowledges the "strong suggestion that the more immediate reaction to any disequilibrium . . . is likely to take in predominant degree the form of a change in the physical volume of activity rather than that of a change in the price level, particularly in the downward direction."

Although Wallace Peterson's (1988b) current edition devotes an entire chapter to Post Keynesian macroeconomics (especially unusual when compared with the major current textbooks, which do not treat the school and its ideas at all), it does not focus on either administered, markup, or target-return pricing. He cites Means and Galbraith as "probably the best-known advocates of the thesis that concentrated market power in the oligopolistic sectors of the economy is a major factor in inflation, particularly inflation when unemployment is high" (p. 456), and does not mention Eichner's work in this respect.

Another current text which devotes some attention to Post Keynesian macroeconomics, Colander (1986), simply refers to Means as the author of an "early cost-push" theory which "focused on the product-market monopolies and the monopolist's profits as the cause of inflation,'' also noting that ''the product-market emphasis was quickly dropped, and for later economists it became fashionable to focus on the labor market and wage-push inflation'' (p. 280). Administrative, markup, and target-return pricing are not discussed.

(iv) The Corporation and Corporate Power

The Modern Corporation and Private Property was very well received. Lawyers who reviewed the book were impressed with the statistical work of Means (see the citations in Stigler and Friedland 1983). Charles A. Beard, the historian, lauded Means's ''wide-reaching, statistical investigations of the highest order'' (Katz and Robbins 1988, p. 212). Maurice Wormser, writing in *The Management Review*, said that the proposition that the separation of ownership and control is the logical outcome of corporate development is ''satisfactorily established by a wealth of evidence'' (Katz and Robbins 1988, p. 203).

Stuart Chase praised Means's statistical work and supported the authors' contentions concerning the separation of ownership and control. In supporting them, however, he brought up, perhaps inadvertently, one of the major criticisms of the theory of the separation of ownership and control:

> Control is answerable to God alone. Its interests may be—and frequently are—diametrically opposed to those of the impotent owners of property. . . . Practically the only curb on control in this connection is that created by *the future necessity of obtaining more money from stockholders through subscriptions to new issues.* (Katz and Robbins 1988, p. 209; emphasis added)

Chase echoed Berle and Means's assertion that the corporation rivals and may soon overtake the state as the dominant form of social organization. He concluded that the corporate giants are ''rotten ripe for collective ownership and management . . . for on the smooth functioning of two hundred corporations, our community life depends'' (Katz and Robbins 1988, p. 210).

Nor were reviewers ignorant of the implications of the book for economic theory. Beard concluded that "when the theory of political economy is set over against the hard facts . . . described above, the unreality of the theory becomes apparent to any one who can think at all" (Katz and Robbins 1988, p. 213).

The reviewers were not without criticism, however. Wormser, in perhaps the most critical review, took issue with two of Berle and Means's assertions. Wormser first claimed that the common law is sufficiently adaptable to deal with any problems due to the abuse of managerial power (Katz and Robbins 1988, pp. 203–204). Wormser next disputed the authors' assertion that the state will be overtaken by the corporation as the dominant form of social organization, calling this theory "applesauce" (Katz and Robbins 1988, p. 205).

The economist reviewers were also very receptive to the book. Ben Lewis (1935, p. 548; quoted in Stigler and Friedland 1983, p. 244), reviewing the book in the *Journal of Political Economy*, acknowledged the importance of its findings for economic theory:

> The implications of this development challenge many of the basic assumptions of current thought: it is necessary now to think in terms of immense non-competing business units; the principles of duopoly have become more important than those of free competition; . . . and economic forces are being supplanted by the conscious activity of a handful of individuals in the governing and control of production. . . .

Further statistical evidence supporting Berle and Means's assertions about the dominant role of the corporation and the separation of ownership and control was not long in coming. W. L. Crum (1935, p. 283; quoted in Stigler and Friedland, p. 245) analyzed income tax returns to conclude that " a very large part of American industry is subject to control, as respects current operations and long run planning, by executives of a very small number of great corporations."

Robert A. Gordon (1936, 1938, 1940, 1945) provided a series of studies supporting the theory of the separation of ownership and control. In one study, analyzing stock ownership by management and control groups, Gordon concluded that "it seems improbable that much more than 15 percent of the total ownership of these 155 corporations can be said to be associated with control" (Gordon 1938, p. 395; quoted in Stigler and Friedland 1983, p. 246). This statement took on added importance when coupled with his assertion that "the traditional reward of the business leader—the profits arising from business ownership—is not a primary incentive to the majority of top executives in our largest corporations" (Gordon 1945, p. 312; quoted in Stigler and Friedland 1983, p. 246).

On the whole, then, these early reviews were quite favorable, despite their negative implications for economic theory. Perhaps the lack of outspoken resistance derived from the fact, observable later, that the arrow shot from Berle and Means's bow never fully penetrated the armor of orthodox economic theory.

The more recent views of Berle and Means's analysis of the corporation were certainly more mixed than those contained in the early reviews. Robert Lekachman (Katz and Robbins 1988, pp. 215–216) claimed that the book's empirical findings have held up well over the years and acknowledged its influence on Securities Exchange legislation (for a different view, see Stigler and Friedland 1983, pp. 243–244). Despite this, Lekachman (Katz and Robbins 1988, p. 216) recognized the book's limited impact on mainstream theory: "Berle and Means did not, as Keynes did, revolutionize economic theory—at least as the theorists practice its mysteries."

Moreover, merely to examine the questions posed by Berle and Means about the role of the corporation and of government vis-à-vis the corporation shows "what a very short distance has been traveled toward explicit and acceptable redefinition of the corporation's legitimate role" (Katz and Robbins 1988, p. 217).

Perhaps nowhere is the distance between the ideas of Berle and Means and modern economic theory so clearly seen than in the *Journal of Law and Economics* collection from the Hoover Institution conference. In the lead article, Stigler and Friedland (1983) launch a stinging attack on the theories and evidence presented in

The Modern Corporation and Private Property, whose publication was being "celebrated" by the conference and the collection. They claim (p. 238) that the statistical evidence presented by Means on the separation of ownership and control was "scattered and fragmentary," though the Berle and Means argument "seemed a valid generalization and one that was becoming even more descriptive with time"; and that support for the proposition that the interests of management and stockholders diverges widely "received no systematic attention" and was inconclusive.

Stigler and Friedland go on to decry the triumph of substance over form in the book: "Means' work was nakedly empirical: he had no systematic theory of the causes or consequences of the separation of ownership and control" (p. 258).

They then present the results of their own statistical examination of the corporation, results said to indicate that management-dominated corporations do not differ significantly from owner-dominated corporations in terms of executive compensation and profitability (p. 252). They conclude that "the main tradition of economic theory was perhaps instinctively recognizing these facts when it continued to work in complete disregard of *The Modern Corporation*" (p. 259).

Writing in the same publication, Harold Demsetz (1983, p. 377) argues that the ownership structure of the firm is "an endogenous outcome of a maximizing process." He goes on to say that "a broader perspective on the problem of the optimum ownership structure makes the fears of Berle and Means meaningless." Finally, Fama and Jensen (1983, pp. 301–302) argue that the separation of ownership and control survives because of the benefits of specialization in management and risk bearing, and because of its effect in controlling the agency problem in large corporations.

The impact of Berle and Means on modern neoclassical theory has indeed been minimal. To the extent that the findings of Berle and Means are acknowledged to be true, they are interpreted as the outcome of the firm's profit-maximizing strategies, something regarded as an assumption by Berle and Means.

Despite the cool attitude of modern neoclassical economists, or at least those of the Chicago School, to its ideas, *The Modern Corporation and Private Property* forms the foundation of the institutional economists' analyses of the corporation. These ideas have had their greatest impact through the work of John Kenneth Galbraith, whose *The New Industrial State* (1967) is a late-twentieth-century complement to Berle and Means's book. Galbraith (1983, p. 131) subsequently emphasized the importance of the rise of the organization as a source of power and the simultaneous decline of personality and property as sources of industrial power. The decline of personality has come about as "the powerful personality has been replaced by the management team; the entrepreneur has yielded to the faceless organization man" (1983, p. 133). The decline of property as a source of power has come about as a result of two factors: the dispersion of ownership holdings through inheritance, and the increasing complexity of industrial tasks which call for specialized management (1983, p. 134). The significance of this transformation for the traditional theory is clear:

> A major purpose of the great industrial enterprise . . . is to restrain or eliminate price competition—to ensure, so far as may be possible, that there is no alternative at a lower price. . . . Thus a primary purpose of organization has been to escape the power-limiting tendencies, otherwise called the discipline, of the market, and this has been widely successful. (1983, pp. 136–137)[57]

Daniel Fusfeld (1979, p. 139) claimed that "the United States has moved well down the path toward a corporate state." A relatively few "supercorporations" dominate both the world and the domestic economy, the result being the use of American economic and political power "in the world at large in the interests of those who manage the emerging American corporate state" (p. 140). Fusfeld offers further confirmation of the Berle and Means concentration of power thesis, pointing out that the largest one hundred manufacturing firms in 1968 held a larger share of manufacturing assets than the largest two hundred firms in 1950 (p. 140).

Furthermore, says Fusfeld, while the separation of ownership and control may have greatly dispersed ownership, it served the more important function of loosening management from the control of owners. The result has been the rise of "a self-selecting business elite whose influence over economic affairs increases with the growing dominance of the firms they manage" (p. 141).

Another important point raised by Fusfeld is that these giant corporations have become "private governments," "in the sense that their actions and policies govern the alternatives open to millions of people and thousands of communities" (p. 141). The pricing, locational, wage, and, inter alia, investment decisions of the corporate giants have a major impact on society because of the sheer size of these entities. The importance of the separation of ownership and control is especially obvious here: much of our life is governed by a small group of businessmen who are responsible only to themselves, who select their own successors, and whose organizations maintain or increase their position over time (p. 141).

In a summary of the institutionalist view of the corporation and corporate power, Munkirs (1987, pp. 1685, 1688–1689, 1695) provides evidence of the influence of Berle and Means:

> the traditional concerns addressed in the market system literature pertaining primarily to resource allocation, efficiency, and abnormally high profits, are extremely important, but . . . the autarchic powers inherent in the economy's centrally planned sector represent a quantum leap, and, indeed, challenge the very essence of the nature of our concept of democratic society. . . .
>
> Regardless of the numerous statistical artifacts or mirages suggesting the existence of competitive market structures . . . our preliminary estimate . . . is that between 55 and 60 percent of the country's goods and services are generated by the economy's centrally planned sector. . . .
>
> Corporate leaders in the economy's centrally planned sector have been very successful in affecting and effecting the government's legislative agendas and in staffing key executive branch agencies with people who profess a belief in the competitive market structure ideology, as well as in laissez-faire . . . and, therefore, with people who are,

> for the most part, simply unwilling to use government institutions as a countervailing power against corporate power on behalf of the general public.

The legacy of *The Modern Corporation and Private Property* lies, at least within economics, in the institutionalist tradition. The fact, however, that hostile, conservative economists held a conference on the fiftieth anniversary of its publication, suggests that what the book had to say on the corporation, corporate power, and the corporate system continues to be so important, perhaps so dangerous, that it cannot be left alone on the library shelf.

9. The Sociology of Academic Opportunity

One question, at once both serious and sensitive, needs to be considered: is the discipline of economics motivated and structured to provide meaningful intellectual opportunity and recognition for those who disagree with and/or write outside its hierarchic orthodoxy, for those who disagree with the received paradigm (however diverse its formulations may be)? What is the response to heterodoxy of those who are antagonistic, on professional and/or ideological grounds, to any perceived challenge to belief in the omnipresence and omnicompetence of the price system (market) and to any affirmation of the role of power in the economy?

Caroline Ware, Means's coauthor and widow, believes that *The Modern Corporation and Private Property* and the rest of Means's work "have been largely ignored and at times actively resisted by the economics profession spokesmen for business and makers of public policy" (Ware 1988a, p. 1). What was unsafe could not possibly be true. She remembers that in the 1930s "some business economists . . . regarded the concept of administered prices as an attack on business and repudiated the concept on that ground" (p. 6). It was, and was seen as, "a rallying point for those who believe that the economy is improperly dominated by business" (DePodwin and Seldin 1963, p. 116; quoted in Ware

1988a, p. 11). Efforts to study how corporate executives determine the prices they charge "were often stonewalled by corporations as business secrets to which only the company insiders were privy" and "economists did not develop tools of analysis to penetrate this area" (p. 8). Orthodox economists are content to assume that firms set output levels and prices by equating marginal revenue and marginal cost. On the other hand, various economists have claimed to have "exploded" and "controverted" Means (p. 6), whereas their efforts did, as she and others see the matter, no such thing.

Ware believes that "for half a century the economic fraternity has turned its back on the implications for macro-theory of the fact that the large corporation is the principal economic institution of modern life" (p. 15). Ware does not lionize Means, though she is no more objective than any of his antagonistic critics.

One very Kuhnian explanation which she offers for what she perceives as the discipline's ignoring of Means's ideas lies "in the defense of the economics profession. No established profession holding a given body of thought willingly tolerates challenges to its basic premises. To admit that prices which equate supply and demand do not provide the essential mechanism of macroeconomic adjustment is to pull the foundations out from under traditional economic theory and to undermine the expertise built on this foundation. It is not reasonable to expect the high priests of the temple to recast their basic doctrine or tools of analysis" (p. 16). Thus, books (such as Blair, 1972) which elaborate Means's analysis, receive "no reviews in the major economic journals" (p. 14), and a leading professional journal refused publication of a rejoinder by Means "alleging no less than seventeen errors of fact or in the interpretation of his position" (p. 13). There is, too, the rejection of the theoretical chapters of the proposed dissertation, a "rebuff" which, as we have seen, Means attributed to "the impervious character of an established paradigm" (Means 1975, p. 153).

A second, alternative explanation for the way in which Means's work has been ignored, which she also finds plausible, is "the influence of corporate power" (Ware 1988a, p. 17). "It is in the interest of corporations to perpetuate the assumption that they are subject to the conditions of the traditional competitive market and to discourage attention to their exercise of market power." Indeed, "if they can be assumed to behave like small businesses without influence over the market they will enjoy greater freedom of action" (p. 17). Ware reports her (and Means's) understanding that General Motors "indirectly secured the determination of the original publisher, Commerce Clearing House, not to re-issue *The Modern Corporation and Private Property*. But this did not prevent the latter from selling the plates to another publisher with a wider system of distribution" (p. 17). Apparently "a member of the board of the original" publisher "objected that the book was anti-business and persuaded the board to sell the plates and publication rights"—ironically, to Macmillan, who "brought out a trade edition which was reviewed on the front page of the *N. Y. Herald Tribune* and gave immense publicity to what had been an obscure legal volume" (Ware 1988b, p. 3; see Beard review reprinted in Katz and Robbins 1988, pp. 211–214).

If it were the case that Berle and Means's original publisher was pressured to delete the book from their list, such certainly redounded to the benefit of the authors. The book became a true classic. Business certainly has, during the last century, attempted to influence the development of academic thought, though not all business has done so.

Ware is undoubtedly correct that received paradigm, ideology, and hierarchic structure are critical filtration mechanisms which serve to exclude, even disparage, heterodox ideas, and that these operate through the choice of books to review and articles to publish. What is not "normal science"—at least as the orthodox comprehend it—is not science and has no place in the discipline. Economists whose minds work within the reigning paradigm need not and do not think twice about ignoring or rejecting the heterodox as wrong if not outlandish, or, more conveniently, as lacking in "sophistication" (read: lacking use of mathematics and the models used by those in the citation- or in-group). At the least, the heterodox is of no interest to such economists. In their view, neither academic nor intellectual freedom is involved, only error—a situation not too different in its effects from attempts by businessmen and others attempting what amounts to censorship of ideas that are repugnant or dangerous. The above description of the discipline is factually true, as has become increasingly understood after the publications by Thomas Kuhn and others working in the sociology of the sciences and the professions.

Means's theories of the corporation and of administered pricing represented a real danger to belief in the price system and its adequacy for social control, and in the cogency and propriety of minimizing deliberative government control. These beliefs are given effect in and reinforced by the orthodox paradigm, so that maintenance of the hierarchic position of those who adhere to that paradigm has the sometimes intended and sometimes inadvertent effect of reinforcing these beliefs.

Nonetheless, this view, empasizing exclusion if not repression, does not fully appreciate several things. First, economics as a whole is in fact diverse. The orthodox are in fact dismissive of the heterodox. And the heterodox tend to dismiss the work of the orthodox as mathematical and/or incomplete and thus incorrect, though harder to ignore simply because it is orthodox. But heterodoxy is alive if not exceedingly well within economics, most notably Post Keynesian and institutionalist economics. Moreover, the publishing business may well be more open to economic heterodoxy than is academia. Still, while economics may be diverse, the prevalent mutual exclusion does not breed synthesis.

Second, even within the more or less orthodox mainstream there is work done which is very different from, indeed contradictory to, the most extreme and exclusivist version of orthodoxy—which often tends to be the Chicago School. Nossiter (1962, pp. 17–18) did not exaggerate much if at all when he wrote that the insights of Berle and Means are "now accepted as commonplace,"[58] and that "in the last few years, no respectable explanation of the new inflation—inflation at less than full employment—has been complete without reference to the market power of firms and unions in industries where competition is among the few. . . ."[59]

All in all, neither the heterodox economists nor their awkward ideas have as yet been totally excluded—though that is not to say that such may be the goal of some orthodox economists and the partial result of widespread practice. For the discipline is driven by status emulation and its operation is channeled by the received paradigm. The desire to be like those economists and departments at the upper hierarchic levels is widespread, certainly among the research oriented departments and even beyond, with the consequence that it is difficult, albeit not impossible, for heterodox scholars to gain secure homes within the discipline.

Third, the interpretive error to be avoided is to identify the discipline (as is so often done by orthodox economists) solely with the orthodox mainstream. The psychodynamic origin of this tendency is the combination of actual rejection by the in-group and the sense of rejection by the out-group. But the discipline includes both in- and out-group. The whole should not be stipulated by the one or the other, or by the margin, even though the margin is long and deep. Alienation should not distort reality on either side of the great divide between orthodoxy and heterodoxy.

Fourth, the world of the intellect, including the world of the mind directed to the definition of reality as a basis of policy, includes, but goes far beyond, economics. Means believed himself an economist, and quite properly. But his intended domain was far greater than that of academic economics. For all the negative response he received from economists (and it is important to recognize that from economists he also received much affirmative reinforcement and great acclaim), he also received acclaim in this larger world. How critical, after all, was the rejection of the theoretical chapters from the dissertation, especially given the success of *The Modern Corporation and Private Property*? Alas, that rejection may well have been critical for Means's perception of himself as an outsider.

Fifth, there is much within mainstream theory which effectively stands as a tribute to Means's challenge to neoclassical economic theory. The large literature on administered prices, while no small part of it is an effort to falsify and discredit Means, is a growing monument to the importance of his arguments—and to sensitivity to that importance within the mainstream. The literature on agency theory, for example, is something of a response to Means, trying to show that the separation of ownership and control is a profit-maximizing response to the corporate situation and, hence, that it is consistent with neoclassical economic theory. Whereas the former literature demonstrates how data can be massaged and interpreted differently within different paradigms, the latter literature demonstrates both the importance of the received paradigm and its utility for showing that anything that exists is efficient or optimal, both of which are question begging. Inasmuch as there is also a large econometric literature which purports to show that administered pricing and an administered price sector do exist, these debates rage on, though seemingly governed more by the search for data and econometric technique which confirm the author's prior conceptions than by the search for "truth." But then economics is very much more a mode of persuasion than a means to Truth, and the contest is much less between facts than between paradigms (stories) within which the raw data acquire meaning or have meaning imposed upon them. Nevertheless, Means has not been ignored; rather he has been honored by being treated relatively seriously.[60]

There is much to be deplored, then, in the treatment accorded to Means (and to others) by the orthodox mainstream of economics. We now seem to know, however, on the basis of work done in the sociology of the sciences and the professions, that such treatment, alas, is to be expected in a wide variety of fields.[61] Such understanding does not excuse deplorable treatment, but it does suggest that were heterodoxy to become orthodoxy, much the same behavior would occur. Alas, again. Whether this would have characterized the behavior of Gardiner Means, we cannot say—though we think not.

10. Means as an Outsider

This brings us to the question of Means as an outsider. Means was a man of somewhat heroic personal and analytical proportions, though he was a man nonetheless, perhaps with feet of clay. We have already suggested that he was an outsider, due to at least four factors. (a) His perception of himself as an outsider was generated in part by his having been treated as an outsider, as someone with ideas so heterodox and heretical as to be beyond the pale of respectability. (b) Means also was very much an individualist by nature.[62] Although he adapted somewhat to the work of others, he preferred to reason matters out on his own.[63] Individualism is something which established, "normal science" accepts only within very narrow limits, notwithstanding its affirmation of individualist ideology. Doing one's own thing is creditable generally only for those with whom one agrees, not the other side.[64] This sociological tendency is true of both those who work within the mainstream paradigm and those who work within heterodox paradigms. (c) Means matured as an adult outside the professional socialization process—in Turkey and in business. The Harvard graduate school socialization process had very little if any personal effect on him. (d) Means was not essentially an academic, though he did teach occasionally and had more or less close personal ties with academia. Inasmuch as the professional or disciplinary mainstream is academic, it is very hard, indeed well nigh impossible, for a nonacademic, and especially a heterodox one, to achieve insider status—though, of course, he did, within Post Keynesian and institutional economics.

There are difficult, if not perverse, personalities within mainstream economics—and Means was not difficult as intellectuals go, and certainly not perverse. The key is the extent to which academia truly encourages dissent while claiming to operate under the principle of academic freedom. Activism deemed "radical" is dismissed as unscholarly, whereas activism in the name of the esteemed is lauded. Nonconformist ideas are placed on the defensive. Means and many other heterodox economists have suffered from this, no matter how much obloquy they may be thought to have brought on themselves. That orthodox economists can say the same things and still succeed is not a sufficient rebuttal, though it does reveal much about the sociology of the discipline.

That the status of Means in the discipline is due to a concatenation of factors is nicely illustrated by the candid and perceptive statements of Raymond J. Saulnier (letter to Lee, 5 October 1987):

> Partly because his [Means's] work was more "institutional" than the Cambridge and Harvard writers [Robinson and Chamberlin], and perhaps less "elegant" in form, I think it is fair to say that Means was [in the 1930s] more on the periphery than at the center of academic debates on price theory at the time.
>
> Gardiner Means was an exceedingly able man, and personally charming, but always something of a maverick, intellectually, and for that reason always out of the intellectual mainstream. He was also a dogged defender of his views, as all of us learned who argued with him on the side of a more conventional (classical) analysis of markets.

It is obvious, then, that correlative to the selective perception exercised by Means in comprehending the modern economy is that exercised by others in comprehending Means himself.

Means's place in the history of economics might have been enhanced by a prestigious academic appointment. Such an appointment apparently was precluded by his evident heterodoxy but also by his personal commitment to government service. Caroline Ware reports in private conversation that Means seemed never to have desired an academic career and never sought an academic appointment. He regarded himself an independent thinker and researcher. Ware reports that Means felt that if he was on the right track in his thinking, then people would listen to what he had to say—an optimistic orientation she thinks derived from the exhilarating experience of the extraordinary reception given to *The Modern Corporation and Private Property*.

6

Gardiner C. Means in the History of Economic Thought: A Preliminary Assessment

Gardiner Means has a secure place in the history of twentieth-century economic thought as the coauthor of *The Modern Corporation and Private Property*, with its emphasis on the corporation, the corporate system, the concentration of industrial power among giant firms, the dispersion of stock ownership and the separation of ownership and control, the transformation of the institution of private property, the economy as a system of power, and the corporation as private government.

He also should be credited with some further specific contributions to economics, the promise of each of which remains largely unfulfilled. He raised the serious question of how the substance of profit maximization is determined within the giant corporation. He established the theory of administered pricing. He helped establish the possibility of connections between industrial structure and macroeconomic performance, suggesting for example, that administered inflation results from perverse pricing. He provided independent, if heterodox, microfoundations of macroeconomics. He raised serious questions about the price adjustment process, along lines not seriously advanced by Keynes. He developed what later became, when restated by Coase, a theory of the firm in relation to the market. He raised these questions and provided his own answers. Agreement with Means on either the importance of these questions or on his specific answers should not be a prerequisite to recognizing that Gardiner Means was a seminal thinker of great sophistication as well as a prolific writer. Numerous orthodox economists have developed substantial reputations on much less credible a basis.

Gardiner Means was a Post Keynesian economist, perhaps the first; and he was an institutional economist. His place in the history of economic thought will depend, then, on the status given to those two schools of economic thought. Means was also economically conservative, indeed remarkably so for someone who has been the object of repeated attacks as a critic of business and of the market economy. We shall consider these points in sequence.

John Maynard Keynes has at least one characteristic in common with Adam Smith, David Ricardo and, inter alia, Karl Marx: his greatest work has been subjected to multiple interpretations. This has been true for many reasons, only one of which is that macroeconomics, including Keynes's macroeconomics, is so complex that many different interpretive handles can be gotten on it. This diversity of interpretation also extends to the question of what Keynes himself "really meant." Certainly one of the topics on which interpreters differ is the role of price flexibility. Whatever Keynes intended to be saying about that—and there is no question, we think, that his emphasis was on the *ex ante* relationship between saving and investment and therefore also on uncertainty—the critical role of price flexibility and the price adjustment mechanism is now evident. This is underscored by the practice of several schools of macroeconomic thought which *assume* instantaneous or perfect adjustment, generally tying this to the rationality of economic actors. It is also underscored by those who emphasize the relevance of fix-price or comparable assumptions.

Gardiner Means was at the forefront of those economists who have questioned the price flexibility assumption and thereby also the unequivocal functioning of the price adjustment mechanism in a context of equilibrium economics. He was also in the forefront of those who advised against conducting economic analysis in terms of preconceptions of how pure markets operate; he favored close empirical study of how actual markets operate. He was also a central figure in the development of the field of Industrial Organization and, perhaps especially, in the extension of work in that field to macroeconomics.

For these and other reasons, Means was the first Post Keynesian economist. He emphasized the need to study the adjustment process, the equilibration process, rather than the first and second order stability conditions of equilibrium. He emphasized the need to consider structural factors operative in the determination of macroeconomic performance. He especially emphasized the role of price inflexibility in the analysis of contraction and inflation. Finally, he emphasized the need to examine what takes place within the firm, especially the giant modern corporation, particularly with regard to the formation of its goals and the process through which its pricing policy is formed as it works out what "profit maximization" means to it. These concerns he contrasted with what he took to be the mainstream approaches, which proceeded largely by assumption and which ignored both the processes and content of microeconomic decision making. In all these respects, Means was arguably the first Post Keynesian economist, and those who have worked under that rubric, such as Alfred Eichner, have followed the path he initiated.

This is not to say that Means was the complete Post Keynesian economist. Judging by the work of such Post Keynesians as Sidney Weintraub, Paul Davidson, Alfred Eichner, and Hyman Minsky, there is much more to the paradigm and the work of that school of thought than Means either contemplated or, certainly, developed. Some of their work is related to standard Keynesian lines of reasoning, and some uses (but is not captivated by) conventional mathematical tools. Some of their work involves developing the implications of radical indeterminacy and uncertainty, and some, the structure and operation of financial markets, especially the role of portfolio investment. The further development of Post Keynesian economics may or may not be along, or include, Meansian lines. But his emphases on such topics as structural variables, the operation of the actual price adjustment process, the formation of what profit maximization comes to mean for the corporation, the relation of the firm, the market, and the microeconomic foundations of macroeconomics, remain avenues open to constructive empirical research and theorizing.[65]

Means was also, for those and still other reasons, an institutional economist. His ideas were not mere echoes of Thorstein Veblen, but he was concerned with the same analytical problems as were Veblen[66] and other institutionalists, such as John R. Commons: the organization and control of the economy; the structural features of the economy; the working out by the firm of its identity, organization, goals, and operation; the macroeconomic consequences of microeconomic institutional arrangements; and, inter alia, the genesis and development of fundamental economic institutions, especially the corporation, private property, and the economic role of government. Institutionalists have consistently refused either to submerge the firm, the corporation, and private property as impenetrable black boxes within an array of dubious assumptions, or to analyze their operations in a mechanistic manner in terms of determinate solutions, equilibrium, and presumptively optimal results. Like other institutionalists, Means believed that economists could not simply take exchange transactions for granted as presumptively Pareto-optimal phenomena. He believed that one had to penetrate the process in which contract terms and other aspects of economic performance were worked out. This he found to be often a process administered overwhelmingly by one party, however much impinged upon by market forces, with a result which the other party could only accept or reject.

Lee (1988c, p. 1), however, finds the claim that Means was an institutionalist "to be an empty one."[67] He maintains that Gruchy (1947) treated Means as an institutionalist "even though he did not present any evidence to substantiate the claim" (1988c, p. 1). Lee's arguments are straightforward and almost persuasive: (1) "Means did not draw upon the works of Veblen, Commons, or Mitchell when conceiving of administered prices'' (p. 26). True. (2) Means had no direct links to individual institutional economists, even those at Columbia (W. C. Mitchell, J. M. Clark, R. G. Tugwell), and did not cite their writings, at least up to 1933. He had not been introduced to the institutionalists' writings while at Harvard, and ''as late as 1938 Means had only read one'' of Veblen's books, *The Place of Science in Modern Civilization and Other Essays* (p. 26). True. (3) With respect to the argument, attributed to Gruchy (1947, p. 478), that Means ''drew upon the Institutionalist tradition when formulating his concept of administered prices,'' Lee argues that this argument collapses because of the lack of supporting evidence. Lee therefore argues, first, that ''Means did not explicitly draw upon the traditional concerns of Institutional economists, such as human nature,[68] culture, business cycles, or the economy-in-evolutionary-change, when developing and delineating the notion of administered prices.'' Indeed, Lee correctly insists, ''the Institutionalist tradition at this time continued to maintain that market prices were arrived at through a bargaining process, although the business enterprises involved in the transactions were large-scale enterprises, and continued to not really question the determinateness of costs of large-scale enterprises'' (Lee 1988c, p. 27).

Means, says Lee, ''completely rejected'' (p. 27) the theoretical framework and analytical tools of traditional economic theory,[69] whereas the institutionalist economists only called for their modification. This is correct in regard to administered pricing, but is not relevant to other aspects of Means's work. Indeed, it seems to us that Means did not reject neoclassical theory as a whole, but rather wanted to add to it or replace a part of it (claiming, for example, that the economy consists of both the competitive price and the administered price sectors).

Moreover, institutionalists have been of two minds regarding their relationship to mainstream neoclassical economics: some, generally the disciples of Veblen and of C. E. Ayres, have considered institutional and neoclassical economics to be mutually exclusive; whereas others, generally in the Commons tradition, have considered them to be complementary. Lee, in any event, concludes that "Means was more influenced by neoclassical price theory which cast prices in the essential role of coordinating economic activity than by the writings of Institutional economists" (p. 30).[70]

Dudley Dillard wrote Frederic Lee (18 August 1987) that "on at least two occasions Gardiner Means said to me or in my presence that he did not belong in my colleague Allan Gruchy's *Modern Economic Thought* [Gruchy 1947] because he (Means) was a theorist and not an Institutional Economist. I think this involves a misconception on Means' part that Institutional Economics is not a type of theory; in any case the point is clear that Means viewed himself as a general theorist."

In contrast, Albert Gailord Hart wrote Lee (9 September 1987) that Means "was an unregenerate institutionalist at the time when we of the theoretical camp didn't give that side enough weight—though Jacob Viner told us to be competent theorists we must make ourselves competent institutionalists. Though Means was hard to agree with, he was valued because he freshened up discussions and made us look hard at points we were tempted to brush aside."

In our view, some of this reasoning, while correct, is either irrelevant or inconclusive. The question is neither whether Means read or cited Veblen and other institutionalists nor whether he considered himself to be an institutionalist, but whether he did economics in the same manner as the institutionalists. All institutionalists, it seems to us, have agreed on the importance of the problem of the organization and control—the power structure—of the economy and its evolution, with the notion of the "economy" defined very broadly to include more than the market mechanistically defined and analyzed. All institutionalists have argued that it is not the market which allocates resources but the institutional-power structure which forms and operates through it. In these and other respects, detailed above and in Gruchy (1947), Means was an institutionalist.[71]

It should also be recorded that Means had enormous impact on post–World War II institutionalists working in the field of industrial organization and on a host of structural questions (see W. C. Peterson 1988b). Berle and Means's *Modern Corporation and Private Property*, needless to say, had a profound impact on those institutionalists, writing primarily but not exclusively in the Commons tradition, working on the theory of property and the economic role of government (including the institutionalist version of the field of law and economics). From the extensive use we have made of Commons's (1950) report on Berle and Means, it should be clear that he both closely understood what they said and was very favorably impressed with it.

Curiously, the view which concludes that Means was not an institutionalist comes close to replicating the argument that heterodox economists are not economists because they are not orthodox economists. That Means, perhaps erroneously, did not consider himself an institutionalist is impressive to a degree, but the fact that he did not cite or personally know or associate with those identified unequivocally as institutionalists is less so. The point is driven home, first, by the divergences among institutionalists, and, second, by the tendency of some in the Veblen-Ayres tradition to read those in the Commons tradition out of institutionalism (which parallels the situation in neo-Austrian economics, some of whose practitioners distinguish between true and deviant members).

Means was very much a loner and thus was an outsider in relation not only to the hierarchically superior insiders within the discipline but also to other outsiders. He was never close to Commons or, apparently, to any of Commons's associates. He had no relation at all, according to Caroline Ware, with Robert Lee Hale, whose work at Columbia law school on the economy as a system of power and mutual coercion was very close to that of Commons and was utilized by John Maurice Clark.

It is an interesting characteristic of orthodoxy that personal individualism is generally much subordinated to the practices and conventions of "normal science," whereas heterodoxy is characterized often, if not typically, by an almost extreme individualism;

and the strength of the former is the weakness of the latter. The orthodox person gains a more coherent sense of identity at the price (perhaps not valued very highly) of losing some degrees of freedom; the heterodox person gains many degrees of freedom at the price (perhaps not valued very highly) of losing, in the minds of others if not in his own mind, a clear sense of identity. Yet even within heterodoxy there tends to be an orthodoxy, and personal individualism is looked at askance.

Means was the perennial outsider. By a straightforward sociological definition, Means was not an institutionalist in that he did not enlist in their ranks and become an insider within this outsider group. Yet by another sociological consideration, Means was an institutionalist because he has been seen as one by those who are institutionalists (the granting of the Veblen-Commons Award being perhaps the foremost example of this). Moreover, by an analytical definition, by which an institutionalist is known by the nature of the work he or she has done, Means was an institutionalist.

Means addressed this matter in his remarks delivered upon receiving the Veblen-Commons Award of the institutionalist Association for Evolutionary Economics,[72] and we can let him speak for himself:

> In my search as a scientist for the appropriate postulates to underlie the macrotheory for the modern economy, I found myself in the camp of the institutionalists. Certainly my studies of the modern corporation, of price behavior, and of the structure of the American economy were studies of institutions. But my drive throughout was to obtain the essential postulates for a new and realistic macrotheory, a new paradigm to displace the orthodox.
>
> I remember my surprise when Allen [*sic*] Gruchy interviewed me as a basis for including me in his book on institutional economics. I had read little of Veblen or Commons and was little influenced by either. I was in agreement with these authors on the nonrelevance of orthodox theory, but for different reasons and with a different focus. I protested to Allen that I was primarily a theorist, trying to develop a new general macrotheory, but wanting to base that theory on the

> characteristics of our actual institutions, not on those of 200 years ago.
>
> Of course, Allen was correct that my studies made a contribution to the understanding of our institutions, and he was justified in placing me among the institutionalists, even though this tended to underemphasize my concern with a new general theory. (Means 1975, pp. 151–152)

Means accepted the Veblen-Commons Award, saying, after a review of the development of his ideas and his recent work on an administrative theory of macroeconomic performance, that he shared with other institutionalists the objective of "high employment and relatively stable prices instead of years of stagnation and misery"[73] (p. 156). Much of what he had to say on this occasion, and in many writings, on the macroeconomy as an already quasi-planned administrative process, resonated well with both those institutionalists who agreed with his diagnosis and his call for indicative planning using meaningful policy tools and those who agreed with his diagnosis but were skeptical of just what the call for planning might encompass. Means certainly found a home among the institutionalists, among those who had considered him and his work part of their own for many years.

Apropos the question of Means as a theoretician, which he obviously considered himself, in these remarks Means indicates that he understood the practical nonexclusivity of theory and empiricism. He wrote that his college training in physical sciences left him indoctrinated "in the scientific method, which makes theory grow out of the results of observation and constantly tests that theory through new observations" (p. 149). This, too, affirms both his practical epistemological sophistication and his institutionalism. He also refers here (p. 153) to his "Industrial Prices and Their Relative Inflexibility" (1935) not merely as an empirical exercise but as "a theoretical explanation for business fluctuations and the Great Depression which rested on the nonclassical behavior of administered prices."

The case can be made that Means was the most dangerous institutionalist of them all. This is because his challenge to neoclassical theory was so strong, his presentations of extensive statistical evidence so especially significant, that members of the mainstream of the economics profession devoted much time over several decades trying to disprove his theories, discredit his analysis of the data, and destroy any notion that he had discovered fundamental lacunae or anomalies in received theory. No other institutionalist seems to have presented such an up-front challenge to neoclassical economics and to have received so much attention by neoclassicists endeavoring to refute or disparage their work. It is, therefore, both ironic and serious testimony that Stigler, perhaps Means's most dedicated critic, has written, in regard to attacks on Keynes, as a general principle that "it is an achievement when others think that one's arguments are important enough to be denounced and demolished. Even to be demolished is better for one's self-esteem and reputation than to be ignored: It requires some ability to excite and especially to outrage one's fellow professionals" (Stigler 1988, p. 213). Means certainly did excite friends and outrage foes.

While it is correct that an "ought" cannot be derived from an "is" alone, positive propositions or statements do have normative implications. This is, at least in part, because "is" statements define reality, while policy implications (necessarily taking a position on "ought") tend to flow from definitions of reality, perhaps reinforcing one or another ideological viewpoint. That is why writers attempt to define reality in a manner congruent with and facilitative of their preferred policy prescriptions. That reality can be defined in a number of more or less conflicting ways only indicates the role of selective perception, at the levels of both "is" and "ought." For example, the quantity theory of money, which like any model includes only certain variables structured in a particular way, and which ultimately concerns (as the dependent variable) the price level and not other macroeconomic variables, tends to define reality in a manner facilitative of certain policy goals and not necessarily others.

Gardiner Means's corpus of writings constitutes a particular, complex definition of reality, and as such is one which conflicts with a number of policy perspectives and reinforces others. Means's work was and remains a threat to the neoclassical conception of the modern Western economy, to the individualist ideology of that economy, and to the conventional monetary *cum* fiscal policy apparatus of most Western governments. If, for example, inflation is not due, or not solely or predominantly due, to an excessive rate of growth of the money supply, then not only are monetarist conceptualizations and policies wrong, but policy measures taken in their name are terribly wrongheaded; and so on. This is especially and most deeply true for what Means had to say about administered pricing, the price adjustment process, and the theory of the firm in relation to the market in a dual economy, for it tends to render nugatory all preconceptions about the optimality of markets and market prices.

Means was thus quite radical, but not with regard to his policy recommendations, only with regard to the depth at which he analyzed the modern corporate system. For his own policy recommendations, which seem so radical against a mind-set presuming a more or less competitive and perfectly functioning market and price mechanism, were not inconsistent with the maintenance of the corporate system, and indeed, like Keynes's, arguably would have functioned to reinforce that system. Given the status quo as he understood and analyzed it, Means was a conservative. If he was wrong in his understanding and analysis, then he was wrong; if he was correct, then others have been wrong. If being conservative means to portray an image of the economy different from what arguably exists, then he was no conservative. If being conservative means to work within, reinforce, and give effect to the already existing economy, then he was conservative.

Fundamentally, Means was challenging neither conservatism nor liberalism abstractly considered, but our most fundamental possession, our preconception of how the economy is at bottom organized and controlled. Means affirmed that "owners should get only the amount needed to compensate them for their risk, i.e.

provide them with a satisfactory return,'' and that ''the rest should go to the controllers as an inducement to the most efficient management and directing of the corporation'' (Lee 1988b, p. 14), a position on how markets ought to be structured that is quite different from—and much less radical than—that of Hayek. Means was challenging the traditional individualist ideology and correlatively bringing out into the open the reality of managerialism due in part to the way in which capital markets were structured.

Notice that he was not taking the position of a philosophical realist here. He took the existing corporate system pretty much as given but not as something imperative. He was saying that so long as we have this situation, then policy ought to be consistent with it. He may have been wrong as to his understanding of the situation and/or what policies are consistent with it, but he was not radical in the sense of calling for systemic or structural (for example, antitrust) changes. His reforms were congruent with, indeed derived from, his understanding of the way the economy actually is constituted, not the way he felt it should be reorganized.

In this he was arguably, albeit not conclusively, more conservative than many institutionalists but no less conservative than most Post Keynesians. As Richard Goode (letter to Lee, 8 September 1987) correctly perceived, ''Means was optimistic about the productive capacity of the American economy and allied himself with others of similar views in Washington.'' If there was something seriously wrong with the economic situation it was that the present economic reality of the corporate system did not accord with standard economic theory. Means did not believe that ''the economy is improperly dominated by business'' (DePodwin and Selden 1963, p. 116), but he did believe that both our understanding and policy ought to take cognizance of what he considered the reality of the business economy in its corporate-system form.[74] Such is anticonservative only to those who have something to hide. Means was, we think, probusiness but without the obfuscatory rationalizations. In his view, if the economy is in fact managerialist, or to the extent that it is managerialist, the individualist ideology, and theories and policies predicated upon its definition of reality, will be wrongheaded and will serve the interests of unrecognized and arguably irresponsible power.

Means was an economist who recognized and accepted the status quo of the corporate system as, perhaps, all things considered, something inevitable. But he was willing to face it objectively and openly, recognizing it for what it was, at least as he saw it, and identifying problems and policy solutions both consequent and, in his view, congenial to it. In this he was unlike most other conservative economists and thus does not appear conservative.[75] But conservative he was. In seeing that the modern corporation may have been inconsistent with, if not an enemy of, the free market and of free men, and in endeavoring to construct policies combating this inconsistency, he may have been the most conservative of all conservative economists.

The conflict between the individualist and managerialist ideologies continues, as does the question of which is correct. As Commons wrote in 1938 (Commons 1950, p. 300), such a world is "not contemplated by the older economic or legal science except as something obnoxious which had to be opposed." If by conservative, then, one means facing up to reality, Means was a conservative. After all, Means did accept "the proposition that administered prices are essential to efficient modern business" (Means to Jerry Cohen, 20 March 1964, p. 8),[76] and the cover page of the document on which he was working at his death carries the statement, "This report is dedicated to the market system and to its full and stable operation" (Means 1988).

To the extent, however, that mankind manufactures its own economy through its definition of reality and policies predicated on that reality, Means's political economy constructed one reality rather than another. Looked at objectively, the ultimate significance of Gardiner Means may well be that the managerialist world of planning is with us whether we like it or not. If the economy is manufactured by mankind through its definition of reality and the resultant policies, Means provided a blueprint for reproducing a particular socially constructed reality, the managerial corporate system—all the while believing that he was dealing with something given, as do most of the rest of us.

To the end, Means asked, "How far is it necessary to go in canalizing the action of big corporate management to bring that action into conformity with the public interest? What role has economic planning to play in a free society? Is the concentration of power in the managements of the large corporations consistent with the maintenance of a democratic society? These are the basic questions which must be faced" (Means in Berle and Means 1968, p. xxxviii). They remain so, and Means performed a significant public service in helping economists and others appreciate that this is true.

Means is thus one of the relatively conservative economists who insisted on the need for economists to comprehend the importance of power and institutions in order to understand how the economy operated. Structure was not everything, but to Means it mattered a great deal.

Finally, Means is significant not only for his place in the history of economic thought, but for what he had to offer the student of the history of economics. Means argued that economists ought to comprehend the significance (for both ordinary and analytical discourse and for both the normative nature and apologetic role of economics) of the continued use of the same words in the face of a changing economy: the language and imagery of individualism serves to obscure the realities of a corporate, managerial economy. Means's work is also significant because it demonstrates the importance of paradigm for the identification and comprehension of "facts" and for the establishment of professional status. Statements of fact and of professional accomplishment are paradigm-specific. Paradigms are also the great filtering device employed in interpreting and assessing the history of economic thought. And the variety of ways in which Means's work has been interpreted as either empirical or theoretical further confirms the difficulty of sorting out the threads of deductive and inductive work that are inexorably combined in doing every sort of economics. Most if not all such ideas are uncomfortable for those safely ensconced in any orthodoxy. They thus echo the work and the career of Gardiner Means and may represent some of his more lasting contributions to economics.

Notes

1. In its attention to structural (and other) factors, Means's work is also related to that of Michal Kalecki but this connection is not pursued in this work.

2. Means was a member of the Consumer Advisory Board while he was adviser to Wallace; his membership on the CAB was a by-product of his work with Wallace. He was employed by USDA until 1935, when he commenced work with the Natural Resources Committee.

3. Means related to Frederic Lee in an interview (31 December 1986, p. 5) that "*The Structure of the American Economy* should be viewed as a more elaborate version of *Industrial Prices.* And *Industrial Prices* should be seen as empirical validation for the arguments made in the thesis." See below regarding what was included and excluded from the thesis. Also, note that Means's chapters in *The Modern Corporation and Private Property* presented statistical material in support of the arguments made in that book.

4. Information contained in the preceding paragraphs was obtained from Blaug (1986); Barnes (1988); Fowler (1988); and various documents provided by, and some written by, Caroline F. Ware.

5. For example, the subtitle of *The Corporate Revolution in America (1962a) is "Economic Reality vs. Economic Theory." The summary of his dissertation begins with the statement, "This thesis presents statistical evidence of a change in the fundamental character of economic organization which has been brought about through the growth of corporate activity, and attempts to indicate certain of the more important changes in the assumptions of economic analysis which this development requires" (Means 1962a, p. 15). Among the indicated changes in assumptions is that from "the assumption . . . in which supply is equated to demand through a perfectly flexible price" to how the "modern corporation . . . has altered the character of the market by making price* not an outgrowth of trading but of administration. Prices fixed over periods of time have replaced flexible prices, and supply as defined by classical economists is seldom equated to demand" (idem, p. 18). In Means's preface to the revised edition of *The Modern Corporation and Private Property*, entitled "Implications of the Corporate Revolution in Economic Theory," he wrote, among other

things, that "developments since *The Modern Corporation* was published have tended to confirm the trends indicated there of increasing concentration, increasing dispersion of stock ownership, and increasing separation of ownership and control," and that "from the economic point of view, the crucial implication of this corporate revolution was the extent to which it made obsolete the basic concepts underlying the body of traditional economic theory which was then the basis of public policy. Wealth, enterprise, initiative, the profit motive, and competition, each was shown to have become so changed in character with the revolution as to make traditional theory no longer applicable" (Berle and Means 1968, pp. xxix, xxxi). Thus: "that Chicago economists have not been favorably disposed to the work of Means should occasion no surprise. Means's work has always strived in one way or another, to develop the implications of denying one or another premise of neo-classical economics" (Melvin W. Reder to Samuels, August 10, 1988). In these respects, Chicago clearly and accurately understood Means; of course, he was anything but obtuse in the matter. As for Chicago, it has tended to understand markets *qua* markets as being essentially competitive (independent, for example, of corporate form); see Samuels (1976, pp. 418ff.); and Reder (1982).

6. "The question of how an economy could be expected to work if prices were really flexible seems pretty academic. It is consistent with nineteenth century theorizing, but bears little relation to the modern economy in which the bulk of prices (including wage rates) are very far from being flexible. Granted that it is possible to create a logical picture of what could be expected to happen in an hypothetical economy of flexible prices, the results would have little direct bearing on current problems. The conclusions reached could neither be tested by the evidence of our actual economy nor could they throw much light on public policy" (Means, letter to John T. McNeill, 7 July 1943; G. C. Means Papers, Series IV, Franklin D. Roosevelt Library; quoted in Lee 1988a, pp. 1–2).

7. "Thus the textbook neoclassical description of the enterprise's price and output policy appears to be falsified by the very great majority of all turnover measured by value, and by the quite overwhelming majority of all individual prices. This has worried theorists far too little and they have not bothered to say much. . . . Nothing, then, except a methodologically false tradition forbids us to say that normal price-setting is merely cost-covering, or loss-avoidance plus a decent allowance for net profit; and that the quantification of the word 'decent' is a purely empirical task" (Wiles 1987, pp. 29–30).

8. If Means had been more intimately conversant with the logic of some contemporary conservative reasoning he might have interpreted the situation as one in which the intensive interests of corporate officials overwhelmed the diffuse interests of workers and consumers, leading to the use of government to promote the former rather than the latter interests. Conservatives, however, frequently apply this reasoning to the welfare and regulatory activities of the state, which they often perceive as "rent seeking," but typically not to the processes by which the fundamental institutions of business, such as the powers of and internal relationships within the corporation, have evolved (and also operate internally). These instead are taken for granted and treated as a notational equivalent of the individual person. On various legal, linguistic, and

economic aspects of the corporation as a "person," see Samuels and Miller (1987).

9. The most current data is presented, for example, in Peterson (1988a, pp. 13ff., 53ff., 73ff.).

10. Fred Lee emphasizes very strongly that Means was the creator of concentration ratios and their use in economic analysis (Lee to Samuels, 21 November 1988, p. 1).

11. Thus, for example, Means distinguished his view from that of Veblen: "It is my impression that in discussing absentee ownership Veblen talks about separation of ownership and *management* and not the separation of ownership and *control*. The two conceptions are fundamentally different and have quite different implications" (Means to Jerome Frank, 27 June 1938; Jerome Frank Papers, Box 33, Folder 472, Yale University; quoted in Lee [1988b, p. 22]).

12. In his preface to the revised edition of *The Modern Corporation and Private Property* (1968, p. viii), Berle says that "the two attributes of ownership—risking collective wealth in profit-seeking enterprise and ultimate management of responsibility for that enterprise—had become divorced." A similar view was offered by Means in chapter 9 of his draft dissertation (1933, pp. 160ff.).

13. This statement cannot be taken too literally, first, because of limited liability, and second, because management is largely insulated from conflicting stockholder preferences. See below.

14. Note that in both cases—with or without Hayek's proposed institutional changes—market exchange will yield Pareto-optimal outcomes. But the alternative outcomes, each Pareto-optimal, will differ. Hayek in effect is arguing that the outcome under his proposed arrangements would be superior—and would be superior because stockholders would be making the decisions, not management.

Another perspective is that of Nossiter (1962, p. 19), in a review of Means (1962), writing of US Steel: "The corporation's customers involuntarily supply capital for expansion by paying premium prices. The passive stockholders have this capital credited to their account—the asset value underlying their shares rises—without further investing."

Still another perspective is that of Berle in his preface to Berle and Means (1968, pp. xv, xxi): "A mature corporation typically does not call for investor-supplied capital. It charges a price for its products from which it can pay taxation, costs, depreciation allowances, and can realize a profit over and above all these expenses. Of this profit item, approximately half goes as income taxes to the federal government, and 60 per cent of the remaining half is distributed to its shareholders. It accumulates for capital purposes the undistributed 40 per cent and its depreciation charges. This is a phenomenon not of 'investment,' but of market power." ". . . a new economic fact: that stock markets are no longer places of 'investment' as the word was used by classical economists. Save to a marginal degree, they no longer allocate capital. They are mechanisms for liquidity. The purchaser of stock, save in rare instances, does not buy a new issue."

15. Galbraith has been, of course, a consistent follower of the Berle and Means thesis. His most recent statement is that "according to traditional theory . . . maximizing of profit is the central and inescapable motivation in all economic life,

and, in the case of the large corporate enterprise, not for management but for stockholders. The stockholders are both powerless and, of course, mostly unknown. The management, in other words, has a powerful commitment to maximizing profits but where its own interest is concerned a surprising and improbable detachment from this commitment'' (Galbraith, 1988, p. 45).

16. In the draft dissertation itself, Means (1933, pp. 173–174) said there were ''two interrelated questions.'' ''First—Are profits the most effective incentive for the conduct of modern corporate enterprise? Second—Is competition an effective regulation of profits where the great modern corporations are concerned?''

17. In his draft dissertation, Means (1933, pp. 166–167) noted that there are ''limits to the extent to which profits'' can be ''diverted into the pockets of control quite apart from the small proportion of profits which they may receive as stockholders.'' First, he wrote, ''If we assume, as appears to be generally the case, that the control wishes to maintain its position, this at once limits the extent of the possible diversion. Except in cases in which control is maintained by a legal device, the stockholders must be kept in a reasonably contented frame of mind or the existing control is in danger of losing its advantageous position. If a fair amount of profits is not earned and earmarked for the benefit of the stockholders, their discontent may encourage some other group to organize a proxy fight and seek control.'' And, ''A second limit arises from the usual desire of control to enlarge its economic power through the expansion of the enterprise which it dominates. Expansion presumably involves the raising of new capital. But additional funds are unlikely to be supplied regularly unless the preexisting supplies of capital have been reasonably well treated—have obtained an acceptable return on their investment.'' Means noted that both of these limits ''are of a somewhat indefinite character but at the same time they are probably sufficiently definite to be recognized by control in specific cases.'' Means thus understood from the beginning the relevance and importance, however limited, of several of the arguments later used against his ideas.

18. For brief critiques of managerial theories of the firm, see, for example, Koch 1974, pp. 37ff. and, in a larger context, Okroi 1988, pp. 88–106 and passim.

19. See the various works of Michael Novak, for example, Novak and Cooper (1981).

20. Means (1933, p. 133) proposed in his draft dissertation to include the second quotation as indicative of Smith's ''repudiation of the joint stock company,'' noting parenthetically that joint stock companies for foreign trade were ''at the time he [Smith] was writing the only important manifestation of the corporation outside of banks, insurance companies, and water or canal companies.''

21. For a selective bibliography, see Samuels and Miller 1987, pp. 313–318.

22. ''The inflexibility of administered prices is itself evidence of market power and presents its problems. But economic power is a much more inclusive concept than is market power alone. It influences the use made of available resources, the safety of the products supplied, the amount of waste products polluting the environment, the conditions of work, as well as the fairness of the wages paid and the prices charged'' (Means in Berle and Means 1968, p. xxxiv). Fred Lee questions ''whether power is more fundamental than administered prices. It is true that administered prices is based

on the firms having economic power in the marketplace; but I do not see it as what really separates Means from Neoclassical economics. Administered prices also fundamentally separates Means from Neoclassical economics.'' Lee believes that it would be more accurate to give power and administered prices ''equal billing'' (Lee to Samuels, 21 November 1988, p. 1).

23. Means, of course, eventually worked for the Committee for Economic Development, an organization of progressive businessmen which was formed after World War II.

24. Institutionalists of the Commons, or Wisconsin, tradition have regularly understood government to constitute a collective bargaining process, the collective bargaining state (see Samuels 1967).

25. The allusion should not be lost: citing the law of corporations as a potential constitutional law alludes to the tendency to call the law of property the effective constitution of England.

With regard to the statement about corporations making every effort to avoid regulation, it should be noted that they also seek regulation, for example of trucking, which Means did not foresee, but which nonetheless strengthens the statement quoted in the text.

26. The text continues: ''Shall we then give them still more power by giving to them any residual profits which corporate enterprise may yield?'' The statement given in the text was quoted in part by the *New York Times* obituary editorial, ''The Very Modern Corporation,'' 19 February 1988, on the death of Means.

27. Tibor Scitovsky (to Frederic Lee, 2 October 1987), has written that as a young theoretical economist in the early 1940s he had ''always been dissatisfied with traditional economics' saying vaguely that prices are determined by the market and never explaining what precisely that means. Apart from Walras' auctioneer, Means's 'administered prices' was the first instance of an economist actually saying how and by whom prices are set, which to me seemed important.''

28. Most economists would say that such prices as those observed by Means in the Turkish market were prices which arose in the market but were not perforce market prices in the sense of there being sufficient diffusion of knowledge to generate the one price for a good deemed characteristic of a market. Means probably would acknowledge that there was some informational asymmetry, but would insist that these were in fact prices generated by trades and that there was diffusion of knowledge even if not perfect diffusion.

29. Raman Pichumani summarized Means as having told him that ''the real free enterprise is what they have in underdeveloped countries, in China or India, where you go to your store, you haggle with them. That is free enterprise. That is free economy. There is no price fixing. You go there, they tell you to pay them ten dollars, you say you'll give him five dollars'' (Ware 1988c, p. 12). A quite unrelated but suggestive statement to the same effect comes from Jackson (1989, pp. 107–108): ''Post industrial society is not Walrasian. It is not like the middle eastern bazaar that approximates the barter exchange model which characterizes the classical Walrasian model of perfect competition.'' Jackson regards ''the outcomes in modern monetary/market economies'' as the products of increasing returns to scale in production,

inappropriability, uncertainty, imperfect and costly information, coordination failures, and, of special relevance here, competition limited in intensity: "The modern economy is a 'supermarket economy'; consumers do not haggle over prices. They take them or leave them. . . . Differentiated products are generally sold at prices that exceed marginal cost."

30. See Lee (1988a) for a comprehensive account of Means's doctrine of administered prices.

31. "I have defined an administered price as 'a price which is set for a period of time and a series of transactions'. The great bulk of prices with which the individual comes in contact meet this definition. When your wife goes to the grocery store, she is faced with a whole series of articles with price tabs. She and others can buy at the indicated price or can refrain from buying. When you buy razor blades the price is usually set and you can buy as many packages as the dealer has on hand. If you want more packages than he happens to have in stock, he will tell you to come back tomorrow when he expects to have some more *but he will not raise the price because the immediate demand exceeds the supply*" (Means to Jerry Cohen, 20 March 1964, p. 2).

32. It is not irrelevant to quote Okun (1981, p. 138; see Hodgson 1988, p. 176): "The hallmark of auction markets is the absence of price tags; sellers are price takers and not price makers. In fact, most products are sold with price tags set by the seller and through a process of shopping by the buyer."

33. "At wholesale the great bulk of items are sold at administered prices. Fixed list prices with standard discounts and special discounts are often used but as long as the standard and special discounts are maintained fixed for periods of time and a series of transactions, the resulting sales are at administered prices. The most important categories of *classical market* prices are in the field of farm and forest products and certain metallic raw materials such as lead and zinc. But in modern industry the bulk of prices are administered prices" (Means to Jerry Cohen, 20 March 1964, p. 2).

34. ". . . I want to make it clear that the presence of administered pricing does not mean the absence of competition. It obviously does mean the absence of *classical* competition, i.e. the competition among such a forest of producers that no one producer has the power to set a price and enjoy a series of transactions. But the absence of classical competition does not mean the presence of classical monopoly. Most American industries fall within these extremes. . . . Also, even if the anti-trust laws were *perfectly* enforced, we would not have classical competition in most of American industry. Administered pricing would still be the dominant form of pricing in this country" (Means to Jerry Cohen, 20 March 1964, p. 3).

35. Fred Lee cautions that the foregoing discussion mixes up "Means' analysis of easy entry markets/industries with his analysis of har[d] to enter markets/industries. The former was his attempt to deal with Chamberlin's monopolistic competition, which he, from what I can see, never really came back to after 1962. In addition, this work really was subordin[ate] to his main concern of large corporations and their impact on the economy" (Lee to Samuels, 21 November 1988, p. 1). Lee believes that Means's easy entry analysis should be considered as a footnote to his main analysis. All this would come out more clearly in any detailed chronological account of the evolution of Means's thought and work.

36. Something like this also is implicit in some neo-Austrian theorizing about the entrepreneur, rather than the market, as performing the coordinating function.

37. Hodgson (1988) also says that "without a theory of rules and norms it is more difficult to explain or interpret the activities within the firm because market adjustments of supply and demand do not occur there. When these activities are explained it is not primarily in terms of prices and costs but in terms of the structures and methods of administration and control" (p. 207).

38. Fred Lee acknowledges that "it is true that there is some similarity between Means and Coase," which he thinks "is due to the fact that both discuss the emergence of the firm/factory/large corporation from a competitive general equilibrium perspective," but he "would not make too much of the similarity since their visions of the operation of a capitalist economy are so different" (Lee to Samuels, 21 November 1988, p. 1).

39. Interestingly, throughout much of his earlier writings, Means used "engineering" as a synonym for "administered," in the sense of "social engineering," not a Veblenian control by engineers.

40. To some extent this dualism parallels that between the individualist and managerialist justification of the corporation discussed above. The mechanistic individualist and passive neoclassical conception both have functioned, in part, to absolve management of responsibility for its actions by denying it effective discretion.

From a different angle, Reid (1987, p. 565) writes that "the theory of the farm, in sum, is a subfield of the theory of the firm. And perhaps that explains the current lack of interest in both, for the very task of management—to coordinate idiosyncratic resources for fluctuating opportunities—means that no specific explanation of managerial structure will be uniquely powerful over a long period of time or across many cases."

41. Lee also writes about the role of transaction prices, especially for a series of transactions, in Means's analysis (1988a, p. 16).

42. More specifically: (1) It is not clear what "insatiable wants" means. Presumably it can mean that consumers have an infinite desire to consume and company managements have an infinite desire to accumulate capital and acquire profits. This may or may not be the case but it is so esoteric and empirically unmanageable an assumption that one does not know how to deal with it. (2) Assuming, nonetheless, that households and managements have an infinite desire to consume and acquire profits, respectively, the point is that neither can be expected to do so under all conditions. Consumers are not likely to spend when, for example, prices may fall or when their future incomes (employment) seems uncertain. Managements are not going to invest when their expected rate of profit is not sufficiently higher enough than the return on their next best portfolio alternative.

43. More specifically, while it is possible for labor to price itself out of the market, the more important factor is that both employment and unemployment are determined by the level of output.

44. Lee emphasizes that Means and John Blair did recognize stagflation long before the late 1970s, through their identification of perverse pricing (Lee to Samuels, 21 November 1988, p. 1).

45. Lee suggests that Means had explanations of inflation in addition to perverse pricing, for example, "inflation caused by increasing the profit margins" (see Lee 1988a). He also stresses that "Means picked up perverse pricing from Blair and thus he also deserves some of the credit" (Lee to Samuels, 21 November 1988, pp. 1–2). Again, many of these details would arise in a chronological account of the development of Means's ideas.

46. Lee believes that Means did not, "at least in the 1950s–75, [see] inflation as cost-push; rather he laid [it] on the shoulders of the corporations and saw it at times as profit-push" (Lee to Samuels, 21 November 1988, p. 2).

47. Lee says of this matter that "Means did not believe that the traditional view of the interaction of savings and investment through the interest rate could bring about full employment. In light of the work he had done on *The Modern Corporation and Private Property*, Means initially argued that because the decision to save was carried on by individuals while the decision to invest was in the hands of corporate management, they need not mesh, especially if the markets for capital goods and securities operated in dissimilar fashions. . . . However by the late 1930s he had dropped all interest in this mechanism because he became convinced that corporate enterprises generated most of their investment funds internally and have no need to go to the security markets, thus negating the traditional role the interest rate played in the investment process. Consequently, he shifted his analysis to the impact administered prices had on the employment of economic resources when aggregate demand changes and to the impact the relationship between the demand for money and the stock of money outstanding had on aggregate demand. In combining these arguments, Means felt he could explain the level of employment in terms of the demand for and the stock of money outstanding . . . " (1988a, pp. 53–54 note 35, citing Means 1947).

48. Eichner (1980, pp. 57–58) suggests that if the dissertation "had been accepted in its entirety and published, it would have been one of the earliest discussions in the literature on the following points: (1) the fundamental difference between oligopolistic (fix-price) and non-oligopolistic (flex-price) markets; (2) the irrelevance of marginal costs for analyzing the process of price formation in the oligopolistic market; (3) the importance of recognizing that it is business firms which invest and households which save as opposed to the classical view that investment and savings are identical; and (4) the weakness of the traditional profit and rate-of-return criteria for direct investment in the socially most productive areas."

49. Means's remembrance fourteen months before his death was that "the voice of the establishment did not want to be challenged" (Lee 1986, p. 3).

50. By a leading econometrician of the period, in private conversation.

51. Fred Lee argues, "in regard to what Berle and Means proved with regard to the operation of the economy, . . . the statistical data in the *Modern Corporation* definitely proved that the American economy was very different from the Walrasian general equilibrium picture of an economy and that this would imply that the American economy would operate differently than a Walrasian general equilibrium economy would. Since the Walrasian picture of the economy was the only picture that economists swore by in 1932 (i.e. at this time neoclassical theory, at least that

taught at Harvard, presented no other theoretical picture of the economy), then it would seem reasonable to say that the facts Means put together did in fact 'prove' that neoclassical theory could not explain/account for the behavior of the American economy'' (Lee to Samuels, 21 November 1988, p. 2). While it appears that neoclassical theory in the 1930s was more Marshallian than Walrasian, in pertinent respects the two were then not all that different (in comparison with how the difference materialized in the 1960s to 1980s), and while we are sympathetic to Means's paradigm, we do not believe that any conclusive proof has been given that would enable the objective, impartial analyst to choose unequivocally between paradigms.

52. Means was unable to secure publication in the *American Economic Review* of a powerful rejoinder to Stigler and Kindahl (1973).

53. Eichner (1980, p. 56) has noted that Means's principal findings were ''largely ignored by academic economists, especially those who view themselves as theorists,'' but that his findings ''have since served as the starting point for those who, mainly outside the major graduate departments of economics, have wished to understand the social consequences of . . . 'the corporate revolution.' ''

54. Tobin (1988, p. 36) writes that Chamberlin ''argued in the early 1930s that pure competition among agents with no control over their prices should not be, could not be, the central paradigm of microeconomic theory.'' ''Neoclassical theorists ignored it, because it was annoyingly intractable in general equilibrium models.'' Tobin also argues that it was ignored by Keynes (pp. 36–37).

Most economists seem to believe that the price mechanism performs economic adjustment and coordination. Some, however, attribute these functions to the entrepreneur (or the entrepreneurial function, as it were). The former is dominant, the latter has a more or less marginal place. Apropos of his own work, Coase (1988, p. 37) has written, ''In view of the fact that, while economists treat the price mechanism as a co-ordinating instrument, they also admit the co-ordinating function of the 'entrepreneur,' it is surely important to enquire why co-ordination is the work of the price mechanism in one case and of the entrepreneur in another.'' Means would have agreed, with a passion.

55. Albert Gailord Hart (letter to Lee, 9 September 1987), reports that certain undergraduate teaching materials (''devised by Henry Simons and Aaron Director and freely cribbed by George Stigler and others'') at Chicago in the 1930s ''contrasted the results of free competitive markets and those of a *cartel.* The cartel price was pictured as 'administered'. I can't remember that students ever heard of Means in this connection.'' On the other hand, Martin Bronfenbrenner (letter to Lee, 4 September 1987) reports that at the graduate level at Chicago in the late 1930s, Means's ideas were somewhat alive, ''since Henry Simons agreed with Means that administered prices were delaying recovery and should come down. (But Simons was already more down on trade-union wages than on industrial prices.)''

56. Chamberlin's and Robinson's work was intended to substantially replace orthodox price theory, but that aspect was soon excised. Their basic theories of noncompetitive markets became the core of an added, not a substituted, chapter; and their marginalist techniques were used to further develop and reinforce the standard analysis.

57. The similarity of the underlying idea to Coase's theory of the firm in relation to the market seems obvious, and ironic.

58. Regarding the view of those who found Berle and Means to have provided a rallying point for those critical of business domination, Nossiter continues that the insights of Berle and Means "provided a rationale for the heightened Government intervention of the New Deal and freshened the spirit of regulation then in the air" (Nossiter 1962, p. 17).

59. In the quarter century since Nossiter wrote, the situation in economics has changed: neo-Walrasian, rational expectations, supply-side, and new classical economics all tend to have assumptions (for example, regarding the operation of the price mechanism and the market) which constitute a movement away from the view quoted in the text. Yet economics remains diverse.

60. The point that neoclassical economists have not ignored Means should not be taken out of context; otherwise it would be overly broad and misleading. Lee insists that, "First of all, Means is not taught to graduate students in their theory courses; secondly, when Means is dealt with in I.O. [Industrial Organization] courses, it is generally done so in a very misleading manner; and finally, neoclassical economists have only dealt with Means in a very distorted manner, in particular they ignored his statements and arguments which said that neoclassical economics needs to be replaced by something new. . . . Neoclassical economists have really only dealt with a very narrow aspect of Means's work—i.e. administered prices/inflation—and have done so through the rose tinted lenses of neoclassical price theory. Thus, while neoclassical economists have paid attention to Means, they have only dealt with a small part of his work and have done so with the presupposition that it was wrong and 'we are going to show that.' Hence not only has much of Means's work been ignored, what has been dealt with has been grossly distorted" (Lee to Samuels, 21 November 1988, p. 2).

61. See the symposium in *Research in the History of Economic Thought and Methodology*, vol. 4, 1986, and the references given there.

62. Ware indicated in an interview with Samuels (2 April 1988) that Means was close to certain individuals, especially John Blair, but that he was generally a loner. He was also both a perfectionist and a procrastinator, but dedicated and serious, with a sense that what he was doing was important. Ware says that Means found that neoclassical economics neglected power, which was an important topic to him. But, she says, Means was an independent thinker: he did not keep up with the standard literature. Apropos of Keynes, Ware says that Means seems to have thought of him as a competitor who had captured the broader intellectual community which he, Means, could equally well have done. However, he had not promoted his work so as to try to capture the attention of that community, believing instead in his work and that people are reasonable and will, when they see the value of his work, operate on the basis of that perception. Ware saw both self-confidence and optimism.

63. Richard Goode (letter to Lee, 8 September 1987) wrote that "Means had an original mind and preferred to work matters out for himself and in conversation rather than by extensive reading." Lee (1988a, pp. 43–44 note 13, quoting a letter from Means to Bronfenbrenner, 5 October 1953) argues that while stung by comments from

critics to the effect that he neglected the work of Chamberlin and Robinson, "Means attempted to fashion an explanation of administered prices based on traditional monopoly analysis but without utilizing the marginalist apparatus associated with the Chamberlin-Robinson theories . . . his own experience as a monopolistic competitor led him to reject the relevance of Chamberlin's theory as early as 1934 . . . and, moreover, since he completely rejected marginalism: 'My own hunch is that the current marginalist theory of business behavior as applied to conditions of imperfect competition will ultimately be put in a museum along with the dodo and the theory of consumer surplus.' . . . "

At a "remembrance party" for Means, one speaker, Alvaine Hamilton, was quoted as having written that Means "needed nothing except his chair, by the fireplace, a clipboard, paper, and pencils—and his busy brain! How often I have wished I could pare things down to a few basics and tackle a problem in this kind of ivory tower!" (Ware 1988c, p. 2). The irony of contrasting this picture with the view of Means as economic realist (not in the sense of philosophical realism) is manifest. Indeed, the obituary editorial in the *New York Times* (19 February 1988) speaks of Means as "no ivory tower economist . . . ," a view affirmed by Helmut Arndt in a letter read at the remembrance party (Ware 1988c, p. 6). Betty McCarthy is quoted as having called attention to Means's "unfailing optimism" and "his unassuming manner," his "ability to turn out important work without becoming self-important" (Ware 1988c, p. 13). Being an "individualist" obviously has various possible nuances. John M. Blair once wrote that "the greatest obstacle to his [Means's] wider acceptance in the academic community is Gardiner Means himself" (Blair to Howard Ross, 4 October 1965; Blair papers; we are indebted to Frederic Lee for a copy of this letter). Interestingly, Eli Ginzberg (letter to Lee, 14 September 1987), wrote that upon meeting Means in 1932 at a seminar on what was soon to appear as *The Modern Corporation and Private Property*, he was "unsettled by his brashness. He put himself—or the book—in the same class with Smith's *Wealth of Nations*."

64. Coases's strictures against "blackboard economics" would seem to have had negligible effect, if any, on orthodox practice and belief. But whereas his protestations might be taken with a patronizing chuckle as idiosyncratic, the same coming from a heterodox economist would be taken as evidence of incompetence and the status of a noneconomist.

65. Caroline Ware is sensitive to the designation of her late husband as a Post Keynesian economist. She finds the designation misleading because Means's work was both prior to and simultaneous with that of Keynes's *General Theory* and because of their difference with regard to the role of price inflexibility. The point of the text, however, is that "Post Keynesian" does not refer to derivation from Keynes per se but to a broadly defined school of contemporary economic thought which focuses on, among other things, administered pricing (Alfred Eichner's markup pricing, for example). Use of the term "Post Keynesian" is not intended as a denial of the fact that Means carried out prior and simultaneous work with respect to the *General Theory*; certainly Means was not "post" in regard to Keynes, quite aside from the fact that Means outlived Keynes. The price inflexibility issue separating Means and

Keynes is treated in chapter 4 and Caroline Ware has no objection to that interpretation.

For his part, in contrast to our argument that Means was the first Post Keynesian, Fred Lee "would rather say that Means laid part of the foundations of Post Keynesian micro/macro theory. Thus Means provided some of the roots of Post Keynesian theory but he himself was not Post Keynesian. This distinction should be kept in mind, since the term Post Keynesian was thought up when Means was 75 years old and applied to a group of economists who were half his age" (Lee to Samuels, 21 November 1988, p. 3). Surely this is true, but two further points are relevant. First, no single person provided all the Post Keynesian analysis, so that the argument which Lee makes apropos of Means could be made about Sidney Weintraub, Alfred Eichner, Paul Davidson, and the others. Second, by saying that Means was an institutionalist and a Post Keynesian, we are not trying to identify membership in learned societies but to assign interpretive significance. Means was not an institutionalist with respect to his having borrowed directly from the institutionalists in regard to his initial analyses of administered prices; nor did he then think of himself as an institutionalist. But, as we discuss below, his work was in the institutionalist vein and he did accept the Veblen-Commons Award from the institutionalist society, the Association for Evolutionary Economics. There was, of course, no "Post Keynesian" economics in the early 1930s, but Means's formulation was very much along the lines which Post Keynesian economics eventually developed and his work was used by some Post Keynesian economists.

66. For example, in an essay originally published in 1908, Veblen (1919, p. 219) wrote that "the gravest consequence" of the employment of corporate securities "is the dissociation of ownership from the control of the industrial equipment, whereby the owners of certain securities, which stand in certain immaterial, technical relations to certain other securities, are enabled arbitrarily to control the use of the industrial equipment covered by the latter."

67. Caroline Ware makes some of the same objections as Lee, arguing that Means was an independent thinker and did not consciously follow in the tradition of Veblen et al.

68. The role of human nature is at least implicit in Means's analyses of the separation of ownership and control, and the formation of the substance of the firm's objective function.

69. Means believed that neoclassical tools could be applied to the competitive sector, except insofar as prices were administered.

70. Means, along with most if not all other institutionalists, understood both price, or price mechanism, and institutions as performing the coordination function.

71. In commenting on the foregoing discussion of his interpretation, Fred Lee writes: "My argument that Means was not an institutionalist was made in the context of the origin of the concept of administered prices and in the context of *The Modern Corporation.* In this sense he was not an institutionalist of the kind found around 1930; although his work certainly made him something of a fellow traveler. When you say that Means was an institutionalist, in spite of his protestations, are you not verging on intellectual imperialism[?] Is it not possible for an individual to work in

an institutionalist vein without being one[?] . . . I think a better tack to take is that over the years since 1932 there was a convergence between Means and the institutionalists in terms of characterizing the American economy and its their [*sic*] convergence which makes institutionalists believe that Means was an institutionalist. (This view also suggests that institutionalism became more Meansian in the process.)'' (Lee to Samuels, 21 November 1988, pp. 2–3.) The text makes clear that we believe that Means and the other institutionalists shared certain fundamental conceptions. That Means made contributions to institutionalism is very much apposite to our argument, though Lee is substantially correct as to the content of institutionalist thought around 1930—although the same argument could be made about any of Veblen's or Commons's writings at the time just prior to their publication. With regard to the imperialism argument, as this is written (March 1989), prospective government fees (or fee increases) are interpreted in terms of the ''duck test'': what looks like a duck, walks like a duck, and sounds like a duck, is a duck.

72. The fact that Means was given the Veblen-Commons Award says something of the attitude toward him of the Association for Evolutionary Economics, the institutionalist organization. The fact that he accepted the award says something either about his attitude toward institutionalism or about his desire for recognition per se.

73. These goals are hardly limited, of course, to Means and the institutionalists.

74. Means wrote:

> My major hope has been that I could outline a course of development which on the one hand recognized the inadequacies of the modern mechanism to deal with the problems produced by modern technology and industrial organization and on the other presented a pattern of coordination which could function within a democracy and which would avoid the dictatorial extremes of either fascism or communism. We hear so much to the effect that one must either go back to small scale enterprise or else choose between fascism and communism. I am trying to outline a non-dictatorial technique of economic coordination within which the market can be employed as a useful tool. This is a normal function of government—it is the function which the government has carried on traditionally in supporting the sanctity of contracts and private property i.e. [*sic*] it has already been maintained that if the government would set up conditions in which the contracts and property of individuals were inviolable and yet left to the individual activity in his own interest within this framework of contract and property, then the economy would function effectively. What I am suggesting is setting up an additional framework which supplements the contractual and property framework so as to produce the results the contractual and property framework alone fails to accomplish. It is an amusing prospect of such a proposal that the communists will call such a proposal fascism and business interests will call such a proposal socialism or communism. Of course, it would be neither. (Means to Walter Lippmann, 7 February 1935, quoted in Lee 1987, pp. 39–40)

Orthodox economics tends very strongly to assume that markets alone produce the resulting optimal solutions, or that the results will be optimal; or that private pursuit of self-interest, within the existing system and structure, will satisfy the social interest; that is, that markets and markets alone (moved by self-interest, of course) will suffice. But even within orthodoxy there is the view that markets require a proper set of institutions in order that desirable results may ensue. In other words, the "invisible hand" is not, or not only, the market, but also institutions, including law.

75. Paul Sweezy (letter to Lee, 10 February 1987, quoted in Lee 1988d, p. 22) wrote of Means, "Of course, we had differences: he was a liberal and I a Marxist. . . ." Means wanted to pay attention to "power and who makes what decisions." He concluded that "the corporate system in the United States thus gives a freedom and flexibility and room for independent initiative far in excess of that in Russia. It is the great advantage of free enterprise and the traditional basis of our democratic society" (Berle and Means 1968, pp. xxxvii, xxxviii).

76. As Lee (1988a, p. 56 note 39) points out, "During the 1930s [and beyond], Means disagreed with those structural reformers, generally referred to as neo-Brandeisians, who sought to revitalize the American economy by breaking up corporate enterprises and making prices more flexible and less amenable to administrative control." Means seemed, therefore, to have ended up with a view of executives of the giant modern corporations as "the uncrowned kings and economic masters of the land" (Means 1933, p. 173). But he and Berle seemed always to question the role of the functionless stockholder (Berle and Means 1968, p. xxiii).

References

Notes: Correspondence to F. S. Lee and to W. J. Samuels cited in the text are not listed separately. They may be acquired from Lee at Roosevelt University, Chicago, or Samuels at Michigan State University, East Lansing.

Ackley, G. 1961. *Macroeconomic Theory*. New York: Macmillan.

Atkins, W. E., D. W. McConnell, C. D. Edwards, C. Raushenbush, A. A. Friedrich, and L. S. Reed. 1931. *Economic Behavior: An Institutional Approach.* Boston: Houghton Mifflin.

———. 1939. *Economic Behavior: An Institutional Approach.* Rev. ed. New York: Houghton Mifflin.

Awh, R. 1976. *Microeconomics.* New York: John Wiley & Sons.

Bain, J. S. 1968. *Industrial Organization.* 2d ed. New York: John Wiley & Sons.

Barnes, G. 1988. Obituary. *The Washington Post*, 17 February 1988, p. B6.

Berle, A. A., and G. C. Means. 1932. *The Modern Corporation and Private Property.* New York: Commerce Clearing House.

———. 1933. *The Modern Corporation and Private Property.* New York: Macmillan.

———. 1968. *The Modern Corporation and Private Property.* Rev. ed. New York: Harcourt, Brace & World.

Blair, J. M. 1965. Letter to Howard Ross. 4 October 1965. Blair Papers. 1p.

———. 1972. *Economic Concentration.* New York: Harcourt Brace Jovanovich.

Blair, J. M., G. C. Means, P. S. Florence, J. B. Dirlam, H. Arndt, H. W. de Jong, N. T. Dodge, and A. E. Kahn. 1975. *The Roots of Inflation.* New York: Burt Franklin.

Blair, R., and L. Kenny. 1987. *Microeconomics with Business Applications.* New York: John Wiley & Sons.

Blaug, M. 1986. *Who's Who in Economics.* 2d ed. Cambridge: The MIT Press.

Bonbright, J. G., and G. C. Means. 1932. *The Holding Company: Its Public Significance and its Regulation.* New York: McGraw-Hill.

Bronfenbrenner, M. 1988. *Keizaigaku Tokoro-Dokoro (Here and There in Economics)*. Tokyo: Aoyama Gakuin University, School of International Politics, Economics and Business.
Burnham, J. 1941. *The Managerial Revolution: What Is Happening in the World*. New York: John Day.
Carroll, T. 1983. *Microeconomic Theory: Concepts and Applications*. New York: St. Martin's.
Carter, W. H., and W. Snavely. 1961. *Intermediate Economic Analysis*. New York: McGraw-Hill.
Chambers, E. J. 1961. *Economic Fluctuations and Forecasting*. Englewood Cliffs, NJ: Prentice-Hall.
Clarke, P. 1988. *The Keynesian Revolution in the Making 1924–1936*. New York: Oxford University Press.
Coase, R. H. 1988. *The Firm, the Market, and the Law*. Chicago: University of Chicago Press.
Colander, D. 1986. *Macroeconomics*. Glenview, IL: Scott, Foresman.
Commons, J. E. 1950. *The Economics of Collective Action*. New York: Macmillan.
Crum, W. L. 1935. "The Concentration of Corporate Control." *Journal of Business* 8:269–283.
Demsetz, H. 1983. "The Structure of Ownership and the Theory of the Firm." *Journal of Law and Economics* 26:375–390.
DePodwin, H. J., and R. T. Selden. 1963. "Business Pricing Policies and Inflation." *Journal of Political Economy* 71:116–127.
Dimock, M. E. 1961. *Business and Government*. 4th ed. New York: Holt, Rinehart & Winston.
Drucker, P. F. 1946. *Concept of the Corporation*. New York: John Day.
Eichner, A. S. 1980. "Portrait: Gardiner C. Means." *Challenge* 23, 1:56–59.
Estey, J. A. 1956. *Business Cycles*. Englewood Cliffs, NJ: Prentice-Hall.
Fama, E. F., and M. C. Jensen. 1983. "Separation of Ownership and Control." *Journal of Law and Economics* 26:301–325.
Feiwel, G. R. 1988. Book Review. *Journal of Economic Literature* 26, 4:1740–1742.
Ferry, W. H. 1964. "Irresponsibilities in Metropolitan America." In *The Corporation Take-over*. A. Hacker, ed., 108–121. New York: Harper & Row.
Fowler, G. 1988. Obituary. *New York Times*, 18 February 1988, p. B10.
Friedman, B. 1988. "Evolution Prevails." *Challenge* 31, 4:47–52.
Fusfeld, D. R. 1979. "The Rise of the Corporate State in America." In *The Economy as a System of Power*. Vol. 1. W. J. Samuels, ed., 139–160. New Brunswick, NJ: Transaction Books.
Galbraith, J. K. 1967. *The New Industrial State*. Boston: Houghton Mifflin.
———. 1983. *The Anatomy of Power*. Boston: Houghton Mifflin.
———. 1988. "Big Shots." *The New York Review of Books*, 12 May 1988, pp. 44–47.
Garb, G. 1981. *Microeconomics: Theory, Applications, Innovations*. New York: Macmillan.

Gordon, R. A. 1936. "Shareholdings of Officers and Directors in American Industrial Corporations." *Quarterly Journal of Economics* 50:622–657.

———. 1938. "Ownership by Management and Control Groups in the Large Corporations." *Quarterly Journal of Economics* 52:367–400.

———. 1940. "Ownership and Compensation as Incentives to Corporate Executives." *Quarterly Journal of Economics* 54:455–473.

———. 1945. *Business Leadership in the Large Corporation.* Washington, DC: Brookings.

Grampp, W. D. 1986. "Evolution and Revolution in the History of Economics." Presented at Annual Meeting of History of Economics Society, New York, 2–4 June 1986.

Greer, D. F. 1980. *Industrial Organization and Public Policy.* New York: Macmillan.

Gruchy, A. G. 1947. *Modern Economic Thought: The American Contribution.* New York: Prentice-Hall.

Hartley, K., and C. Tisdell. 1981. *Microeconomic Policy.* New York: John Wiley & Sons.

Hayek, F. A. 1967. "The Corporation in a Democratic Society: In Whose Interest Ought It To and Will It Be Run?" In *Studies in Philosophy, Politics and Economics.* F. A. Hayek, ed., 300–312. Chicago: University of Chicago Press.

Heilbroner, R. L. 1988. *Behind the Veil of Economics.* New York: Norton.

Hirschleifer, J. 1988. *Price Theory and Applications.* 4th ed. Englewood Cliffs, NJ: Prentice-Hall.

Hodgson, G. M. 1988. *Economics and Institutions.* Philadelphia: University of Pennsylvania Press.

Jackson, P. M. 1989. "The Boundaries of the Public Domain." In *Fundamentals of the Economic Role of Government.* W. J. Samuels, ed. Westport, CT: Greenwood.

Katz, B. S., and R. E. Robbins. 1988. *Modern Economic Classics—Evaluations Through Time.* New York: Garland.

Keynes, J. M. 1926. *Laissez-faire and Communism.* New York: New Republic.

———. 1936. *The General Theory of Employment, Interest and Money.* New York: Harcourt, Brace & World.

Keyserling, L. H. 1987. "Gardiner C. Means." In *The New Palgrave Dictionary of Economics.* Vol. 3. J. Eatwell, M. Milgate, and P. Newman, eds., 421–422. New York: Stockton Press.

Koch, J. V. 1974. *Industrial Organization and Prices.* Englewood Cliffs, NJ: Prentice-Hall.

Kregel, J. A. 1980. "Markets and Institutions as Features of a Capitalistic Production System." *Journal of Post Keynesian Economics* 3:32–48.

Lanzillotti, R. 1958. "Pricing Objectives in Large Companies." *American Economic Review* 48:921–940.

Lee, F. S. 1984. "Whatever Happened to the Full-Cost Principle (USA)?" In *Economics in Disarray.* P. Wiles and G. Routh, eds., 233–239. New York: Basil Blackwell.

———. 1986. Interview with Gardiner C. Means. 31 December 1986. 6pp.
———. 1987. "A New Dealer in Agriculture: G. C. Means and the Writing of *Industrial Prices.*" Working Paper.
———. 1988a. "G. C. Means's Doctrine of Administered Prices." Working Paper.
———. 1988b. "G. C. Means and *The Modern Corporation.*" Working Paper.
———. 1988c. "G. C. Means and the Origin of Administered Prices." Working Paper.
———. 1988d. "Creating Economic Knowledge for National Economic Planning: G. C. Means's Work at the National Resources Committee." Working Paper.
———. 1988e. "Schisms in Economic Theory and Policy in the Latter Years of the New Deal: Gardiner Means and the Keynesians." Working Paper.
Lewis, B. W. 1935. "Berle and Means on the Modern Corporation." *Journal of Political Economy* 43:548–554.
Lindblom, C. 1977. *Politics and Markets*. New York: Basic Books.
McKibbin, R. 1989. "Extravagance." *London Review of Books*, 2 February, pp. 5–6.
Mansfield, E. 1985. *Microeconomics: Theory and Applications*. 5th ed. New York: Norton.
Martin, S. 1988. *Industrial Economics*. New York: Macmillan.
Means, G. C. 1930. "The Diffusion of Stockownership in the United States." *Quarterly Journal of Economics* 44:561–600.
———. 1933. "The Corporate Revolution." Manuscript of Ph.D. dissertation, Harvard University. Gardiner C. Means Papers, Series I. Franklin D. Roosevelt Library.
———. 1935. *Industrial Prices and Their Relative Inflexibility*. Senate Document No. 13, 74th Congress, 1st Session. Washington, DC: United States Government Printing Office.
———. 1935. Letter to Walter Lippman. 7 February 1935. Gardiner C. Means Papers, Series I, Franklin D. Roosevelt Library.
———. 1938. *Patterns of Resource Use*. Washington, DC: Natural Resources Committee, United States Government Printing Office.
———. 1938. Letter to Jerome Frank. 27 June 1938. Jerome Frank Papers, Box 33, Folder 472, Yale University.
———. 1939. *The Structure of the American Economy*. Washington, DC: Natural Resources Committee, United States Government Printing Office.
———. 1943. Letter to John T. McNeill. 7 July 1943. G. C. Means Papers, Series IV. Franklin D. Roosevelt Library.
———. 1947. A Monetary Theory of Employment. Manuscript. Gardiner C. Means Papers, Franklin D. Roosevelt Library. c. 249pp.
———. 1953. Letter to Martin Bronfenbrenner. 5 October 1953. Gardiner C. Means Papers, Franklin D. Roosevelt Library.
———. 1962a. *The Corporate Revolution in America*. New York: Collier.
———. 1962b. *Pricing Power and the Public Interest*. New York: Harper.

———. 1964a. "Collective Capitalism and Economic Theory." In *The Corporation Take-over.* A. Hacker, ed., 65–90. New York: Harper & Row.

———. 1964b. Letter to Jerry Cohen. 20 March 1964. John M. Blair Papers. National Archives. 9pp.

———. 1975. "The Veblen-Commons Award." *Journal of Economics Issues* 9:147–157.

———. 1976. "Which Was the True Keynesian Theory of Employment?" *Challenge* 19, 3:61–63.

———. 1988. "The New Non-Monetary Source of Inflation and Its Elimination." Manuscript.

———. (Undated). Letter to John Blair. 19 December. John M. Blair Papers. National Archives. 3pp.

Means, G. C., and C. F. Ware. 1936. *The Modern Economy in Action.* New York: Harcourt, Brace.

Milgate, M. 1988. Book Review. *Journal of Economic Literature* 26, 4:1747–1748.

Moore, T. G., ed. 1983. "Corporations and Private Property." *Journal of Law and Economics* 26:235–496.

———. 1983. Introduction. *Journal of Law and Economics* 26:235–236.

Mund, V., and R. Wolf. 1971. *Industrial Organization and Public Policy.* New York: Appleton-Century-Crofts.

Munkirs, J. R. 1987. "The Existence and Exercise of Corporate Power: An Opaque Fact." *Journal of Economics Issues* 21:1679–1706.

———. 1988. "Economic Power: History and Institutions." In W. C. Peterson (1988b), pp. 27–52.

New York Times. "The Very Modern Corporation." Editorial. 19 February 1988, p. A34.

Nicholson, W. 1987. *Intermediate Microeconomics and Its Applications.* 4th ed. Chicago: Dryden.

Nossiter, B. 1962. "The World of Gardiner Means." *The New Republic*, 7 May 1962, pp. 17–20.

Novak, M., and J. W. Cooper. 1981. *The Corporation: A Theological Inquiry.* Washington, DC: American Enterprise Institute.

Okroi, L. J. 1988. *Galbraith, Harrington, Heilbroner: Economics and Dissent in an Age of Optimism.* Princeton: Princeton University Press.

Okun, A. M. 1981. *Prices and Quantities.* New York: Basil Blackwell.

Peterson, R. 1988. "Industrial Power: Meaning and Measurement." In *Market Power and the Economy.*" W. S. Peterson, ed. Boston: Kluwer Academic.

Peterson, W. C. 1974. *Income, Employment, and Economic Growth.* 3d ed. New York: Norton.

———, ed. 1988a. *Market Power and the Economy.* Boston: Kluwer Academic.

———. 1988b. *Income, Employment, and Economic Growth.* 6th ed. New York: Norton.

Powelson, J. P. 1960. *National Income and Flow-of-Funds Analysis.* New York:

McGraw-Hill.

Reder, M. W. 1982. "Chicago Economics: Permanence and Change." *Journal of Economic Literature* 20:1–38.

Reid, J. D., Jr. 1987. "The Theory of Sharecropping: Occam's Razor and Economic Analysis." *History of Political Economy* 19, 4:551–569.

Rothenberg, R. 1988. Book Review. *New York Times Book Review*, 24 April 1988, p. 40.

Rowan, D. C., and T. Mayer. 1972. *Intermediate Macroeconomics*. New York: Norton.

Salant, W. S. 1978. "Keynes as Seen by His Students in the 1930s." In *Keynes, Cambridge and The General Theory*. D. Patinkin and J. C. Leith, eds., 43–48. Toronto: University of Toronto Press.

Salvatore, D. 1983. *Microeconomic Theory*. 2d ed. New York: McGraw-Hill.

Samuels, W. J. 1967. "Edwin E. Witte's Concept of the Role of Government in the Economy." *Land Economics* 43:131–147.

———. 1985. "A Critique of *Capitalism, Socialism, and Democracy*." In *Capitalism and Democracy: Schumpeter Revisited*. R. D. Coe and C. K. Wilber, eds., 60–119. Notre Dame: University of Notre Dame Press.

Samuels, W. J., and A. S. Miller, eds. 1987. *Corporations and Society: Power and Responsibility*. Westport, CT: Greenwood.

———. 1988. Interview with Caroline Ware. 2 April 1988. 3pp.

Samuelson, P. A. 1983. "What Would Keynes Have Thought of Rational Expectations? Comment." In *Keynes and the Modern World*. D. Worswick and J. Trevithick, eds., 212–217. Cambridge: Cambridge University Press.

Scherer, F. M. 1971. *Industrial Market Structure and Economic Performance*. Chicago: Rand McNally.

Schumpeter, J. 1928. "The Instability of Capitalism." *Economic Journal* 38:361–386.

———. 1942. *Capitalism, Socialism, and Democracy*. New York: Harper.

Scott, R. 1973. *The Pricing System*. San Francisco: Holden-Day.

Shackle, G. L. S. 1972. *Epistemics and Economics*. New York: Cambridge University Press.

Shapiro, E. 1966. *Macroeconomic Analysis*. New York: Harcourt, Brace & World.

Sher, W., and R. Pinola. 1981. *Microeconomic Theory*. New York: North Holland.

Sherman, H. J. 1983. *Stagflation*. 2d ed. New York: Harper & Row.

Sherman, R. 1974. *The Economics of Industry*. Boston: Little, Brown.

Smith, A. 1937. *An Inquiry Into the Nature and Causes of the Wealth of Nations*. New York: Modern Library.

Stigler, G. J. 1988. *Memoirs of an Unregulated Economist*. New York: Basic Books.

Stigler, G. J. and C. Friedland. 1983. "The Literature of Economics: The Case of Berle and Means." *Journal of Law and Economics* 26:237–268.

Stigler, G. J. and J. K. Kindahl. 1973. "Industrial Prices, as Administered by Dr.

Means.'' *American Economic Review* 13:717–721.
Taussig, F. W. 1930. *Investors and Money-Makers*. New York: Macmillan.
Thompson, A. 1985. *Economics of the Firm: Theory and Practice*. Englewood Cliffs, NJ: Prentice-Hall.
Tobin, J. 1988. ''A Revolution Remembered.'' *Challenge* 31, 4:35–41.
Torr, C. 1988. *Equilibrium, Expectations and Information*. Boulder, CO: Westview Press.
Varian, H. 1987. *Intermediate Microeconomics: A Modern Approach*. New York: Norton.
Veblen, T. 1919. *The Place of Science in Modern Civilization and Other Essays*. New York: B. W. Huebesch.
Vickrey, W. S. 1964. *Metastatics and Macroeconomics*. New York: Harcourt, Brace & World.
Ware, C. F. 1988a. ''Academic Resistance to Administered Prices.'' Manuscript. 23pp.
———. 1988b. ''Some Notes on Gardiner C. Means, Economist.'' Manuscript. 9pp.
———, ed. 1988c. ''Remembrance Party for Gardiner C. Means, May 8, 1988.'' Manuscript. 13pp.
Wiles, P. J. D. 1987. ''Administered Prices.'' In *The New Palgrave Dictionary of Economics*. Vol. 1. J. Eatwell, M. Milgate, and P. Newman, eds., 29–31. New York: Stockton Press.
Williamson, O. E. 1967. *Economics of Discretionary Behavior: Managerial Objectives in a Theory of the Firm*. Chicago: Markham.
Wolfson, N. 1984. *The Modern Corporation: Free Markets vs. Regulation*. New York: Free Press.

Index

About the Authors

WARREN J. SAMUELS is currently professor of economics at Michigan State University. He earned his M.S. and Ph.D. degrees at the University of Wisconsin.

Professor Samuels has written extensively on the history of economic thought, Post Keynesian economics, and institutional economics.

STEVEN G. MEDEMA is assistant professor at the University of Colorado at Denver. He received his M.A. and Ph.D. degrees from Michigan State University.